Lyle G Parker
7-84

HOW I CAN FIT IN

BOOKS BY LAWRENCE O. RICHARDS

A New Face for the Church

Creative Bible Study

How I Can Be Real

How Far I Can Go

How I Can Experience God

How I Can Make Decisions

How I Can Fit In

69 Ways to Start a Study Group

Three Churches in Renewal

Reshaping Evangelical Higher Education
(with Marvin K. Mayers)

A Theology of Christian Education

A Theology of Church Leadership
(with Clyde Hoeldtke)

A Theology of Personal Ministry
(with Gib Martin)

A Theology of Children's Ministry

Discipling Resources Series
(with Norman Wakefield)

Believer's Promise Book

The Believer's Guidebook

HOW I CAN FIT IN

LARRY RICHARDS

Illustrations by Charles Shaw

OF THE ZONDERVAN CORPORATION
GRAND RAPIDS, MICHIGAN 49506

How I Can Fit In
© 1979 by The Zondervan Corporation

First published in 1970 by Moody Press, Chicago, under the title *How Do I Fit In?* Copyright © 1970 by Moody Bible Institute.

Zondervan Revised Edition 1979

Library of Congress Cataloging in Publication Data
Richards, Lawrence O
How I can fit in.

(Answers for youth)
Published in 1970 under title: How do I fit in?
Includes bibliographical references.
1. Youth—Religious life. 2. Interpersonal relations—Juvenile literature.
I. Title.
BV4531.2.R452 1979 248'.83 79-18390
ISBN 0-310-38961-5

Unless otherwise indicated, Scripture quotations are taken from *The Living Bible*, © 1971 by Tyndale House Publishers, Wheaton, Illinois.

Printed in the United States of America

83 84 85 86 87 88 — 10 9 8 7 6 5 4

Contents

1 Reaching out

I sat on the bottom step and listened as Carl haltingly told his story.

"I've been wondering," he began, "if there's something wrong with me.

"Whenever people get to know me, they pull away from me. Like one girl I knew in high school. We went out a few times and we got along pretty well. Then I began to tell her what I thought about things, and to tell her my ideas. And, well, she just seemed to close up and pull away."

It's not a pleasant feeling for anyone—this feeling that you can't reach out and touch other people. The feeling that, when it comes to having friends and being friends, you just don't fit in.

I've thought a lot about Carl and my trip to the small Ohio college he attends. Particularly because I've felt as he did and wondered how to really *belong*. Talking with those in their teens and twenties, I've found many who share Carl's desire for closer personal relationships with others, and who share his uncertainty about how to develop them.[1]

It's only natural to be concerned about personal relationships. "The reason I want to fit in with people," says a sixteen-year-old from Maine, "is that it makes you feel like a part of something and not just a loner. When you have friends, you have somebody to talk to and have fellowship with that person or group. For instance, at school there is a group of kids that I would like to be friends with; but they don't talk to you and then you feel left out, so you just don't get acquainted with them."

A high school girl shared another reason for having friends: "Making them understand how I feel is really important. My parents are extremely understanding when I communicate. My best friend is a crutch, kind of. I use our friendship as a good tool for letting things off my mind in complete trust. My second best friend is of the opposite sex, and that helps me in relating and feeling more at ease with boys in general."

Rick, an Illinois guy who lacked this kind of friendship in high school, must have felt a little like Carl, my Ohio friend. "In high school, I never really felt completely accepted," he wrote. "The kids whom I considered my closest friends had friends who were closer to them than I was. I just never felt that I really had one completely honest, free, and irreplaceable friendship in which there was a giving of ourselves to each other."

A lot of the kids who helped me with this book spoke of the superficiality of relationships they had with others. "I walked with two guys for three years in high school and never got to know them," says a New Yorker. "I was too afraid of many kids to get to know them even casually."

Having only surface-level relationships isn't just for high school, and isn't just for Christian kids. One study of

Stanford and Berkeley university students notes how little disagreement and conflict seem to exist between them, but concludes the reason is not so much "the peacefulness of social relationships as their relative superficiality."[2]

On the surface

What are some of the pressures that keep us on the surface in our relationships with others? Where do teens and youth in their twenties have problems fitting in with others?

On campus. Jay, a college man from Michigan, writes that "The kind of experience that makes me feel a need to fit in is when I'm with a crowd of 'popular' people. I know I don't necessarily have to conform to their standards, but

I still feel uneasy knowing that their standards are different than mine."

Diana, another collegian, knows just what he means: "During high school I always felt I was separate from the other kids, that I was a Christian and they weren't. I felt inferior because dancing, drinking, smoking, etc., were the criteria for being 'in,' and since I did none of them I felt really out of it."

Does becoming active in school organizations provide a solution for how to fit in with school friends? Not necessarily. "I recall being eager to join clubs at school, hoping to be accepted in my group of friends," relates a Florida girl. "I never participated with them much in activities, other than those that were school-related, though I half wished that I had. But then, *I* was a Christian and wasn't 'of the world,' so I comforted myself with this and didn't make any extra effort to become close friends with my high school girl friends."

Relating to kids at school is particularly hard when they are thought of as "non-Christians," and a Christian young person wants somehow to witness to them. "When I was in high school," says an Iowa boy, "I was on the wrestling team. Members of the team would hold drinking parties almost every weekend. I didn't drink, but how could I go to such a party and still give a good witness for Christ? Many Christian teens face similar problems —how to relate to non-Christians without dishonoring Christ."

Many raised just this question. Says one, "In high school and throughout life I find that non-Christians sometimes make me feel uncomfortable. It takes a while to find common ground and a basis for communication that is satisfying to both of us."

And another, "When with non-Christians, especially of

the opposite sex, it's hard to relate friendliness, much less Christianity! I had a moderately close relationship with a non-Christian girl, but I had to break it off because we lived in different worlds."

And, "It is very important to relate to non-Christian kids. Now that I look back I see what a great opportunity high school experiences led to for witnessing, but my problem was that I didn't know how to relate my beliefs to the other kids' problems; because I was unable to communicate with non-Christians, I lost the opportunity. If I only had the ability to communicate my beliefs. . . ."

At home. "I think the hardest thing now," says a college girl from California, "is to be able to get our thoughts and feelings across to our parents; for although they understand, youth is usually quite remote from them."

Two words—*conflict* and *communication*—point up relationship problems my high school and college friends have at home. "I prefer not to talk with my parents," one boy said, "because they are very intolerant of ideas they feel are wrong. So I don't share my ideas."

A girl adds, "Conflicts often arise over the smallest things. I've never been really close to either of my folks. I find myself frequently disagreeing with them over things—I wanted to be open-minded about things which they were closed or opposed to, only I usually succeeded in shutting them out in the process."

This doesn't mean most Christian young people fail to love their parents. The love is usually there. But there are times when all of us have trouble fitting in with those we love. "When I was a high school student," writes Karen, "I had many difficult times in areas of discipline with my parents. Partly this was due to a lack of understanding (not love!) on their part, and a loss of willingness to communicate on my part. This problem was deeply rooted in my preadolescent years when my folks were too busy to listen. Then when things got rough and they *wanted* to communicate, it was too late; it seemed phony to me and I'd lost interest. This is how I realize it now, in looking back. It sure takes a tremendous amount of love and *patience* to keep the communication lines open all through life!"

Of course, many also mentioned difficulty in relating to adults other than parents. "I can't relate to adults," says a college student, "because I feel I have little in common with them. Also, they tend to consider me as I was, and not as old as I am. They can't begin to understand the pressures we feel now (drugs, smoking, drinking) and still treat us as if we don't have a brain in our head. After 'And how are you today?' there's little else said and we both stand around like dopes."

Being uncomfortable with others, uncertain of how to relate, is a pretty general experience. It happens with us at school, with non-Christians, with friends at church, at home with the folks, with other adults. And each of these areas poses some pretty special problems for youth today.

There was one other area many kids mentioned, where relating was felt to pose a problem.

With God. "I constantly feel a need for a deeper relationship with God," wrote one college man. Another collegian says, "If I can't have a close relationship to God then how can I expect to have any beneficial relationship with someone who doesn't love me at all? I've found I can relate more to the unsaved guys on my wrestling team when I am closer to God. If you let God become close to you and you to Him, the other relationships will follow."

Yet many teens and those in their twenties felt they had to admit with this high school girl, "My life as a Christian is not what I wish or want it to be. Sometimes I feel Christ's closeness as a reality, but many times I feel so far from Him."

The need for more than a nodding acquaintance with God and with other people is a very real need. Fitting in and being comfortable with others are especially important for a Christian. The Bible tells us that we need other people and their love, and that they need our love. Growth as a Christian personality always involves growing in our ability to draw close to other people. The way the Bible puts it, letting God have His way in our lives makes it possible "for you to enjoy other people and to like them, and finally you will grow to love them deeply. The more you go on in this way, the more you will grow strong spiritually and become fruitful and useful to our Lord Jesus Christ" (2 Peter 1:7–8).

I guess we all sense it. A need inside, that God has planted there, to draw close to Him, and to others.

Maybe this is what makes us feel so lost inside when we have experiences like Carl's, when we don't know how to draw close, or how to relate to others.

It's good to know that there really are ways, for each of us, to "enjoy other people and to like them"—ways we can "grow to love them deeply."

Steps to take

At the end of each chapter you'll find two or three suggested ways for you to act on what's been said. This book will be more helpful if you jot down your responses.

1. Have you felt like any of the kids quoted here when it comes to fitting in with others? Which ones?

2. If you could, what two specific personal relationships would you like most to improve?
3. Jot down a description of the "ideal" relationship you'd like to have in one or both of the cases you just thought of.

2

Come closer

"I was basically a quiet person when I was in high school," writes a Chicagoan. "I was always on the athletic teams, but I just couldn't seem to relate to the guys on the football team. I can remember walking back to the locker room after Thursday night practice with the guys, but I didn't know what to say. I just didn't know what to talk about."

How can we break through the barrier between us and other people? How can we come closer to them as persons? The fellows and girls who helped with this book offered a lot of advice.

High school and college kids have all sorts of ideas on how to improve personal relationships with others. Some things they feel are important in any relationship are these:

"Listen, really listen, to what the other person has to say," a seventeen-year-old suggested. "So often I interrupt with something I want to say and completely shut down the other person.

Hal, from Iowa, agreed: "I would say be a good listener. Why? Because this makes the person want to accept you more because you have taken an interest in him."

Others saw different purposes in listening: "You must have an understanding of the feelings and emotions of other individuals in order to fit in well. You must look at yourself through the eyes of other individuals around you, and see what personality traits are lacking in your relationships with others."

"I think we should listen as well as contribute to the conversation," said another girl, "as most people seem to appreciate listeners. Also, I'd advise that a person make it a point to discipline himself, to try to be helpful even in little ways, and to please the other person even though it may mean self-sacrifice."

The thought of trying to please others came out in several ways: "If you can sit back and listen to others," said one college student, "even when they really rub the wrong way, and not jump on them, you can develop a much better relationship."

Sometimes the suggestions give the impression that to draw close to others a person has to be a bit deceptive: "I would probably tell a person to always be as friendly as possible and to always have a smile on his face," said one girl.

The way another person put it was simply this: "Control your emotions. Emotions can ruin many friendships."

One person went even further: "Don't criticize or even appear to be critical. Make yourself smile, laugh, be outgoing, even when you feel terrible. Make yourself meet people. Make yourself be attractive."

A lot of kids didn't agree with the "deceptive" approach at all. Jim, a college student, says that it's most important to "be yourself, don't try to be cool or to be like someone you admire to the extent that you lose your own personality. Phonies don't go over well when it's discovered they are phonies. Be yourself; and if certain people don't like you for it, there are more people in the world."

A high schooler agrees: "Try not to put up a front; most kids sense this right off. Being honest with a person is the first step to a close relationship."

To most, the kind of honesty they recommend is a *giving* kind. "Learn to give," said Vi, who goes to a Christian college. "Really open up. Don't worry about how horrible you'll make yourself look. Be honest. But remember that if you honestly open up and expect acceptance, then you must be willing to accept other people who open up to you."

Certainly everyone agreed on one or two things. Getting close to other people takes time, and it takes talk. But it's worth it. As Roy, a nineteen-year-old, shared, "It's so easy to get to know someone on the surface and let it go at that. Only by talking and developing closer relationships can you find out more about that person, yourself, and people in general. I was going with a girl for three months before we got around to having a serious talk. Our relationship after that was beautiful, but I'm still mad about the time that was wasted because we never talked."

The closer you get to others, the more important you discover such relationships to be!

By listening?

This is one of the two most common pieces of advice given on relating: Listen. And it's good advice—to a certain extent, and with limitations.

Listening can be a way of expressing interest in other

people. When we listen because we really want to understand the other person, it always helps.

But probably the big reason listening in this situation helps isn't because of the "technique" itself but because of our underlying motive. Bruce Larson in his little book *Dare to Live Now!* points out that "people respond more to how we feel about them than to what we say to them."[1] This is exactly right! If we're listening as an expression of real interest and concern, people will sense this, and our listening will encourage them to draw closer to us.

But there are many other motives for listening—motives which may be hidden even to us, but which subtly communicate insincerity. The most common is an overriding concern for yourself, and not for the other person.

"In high school," says a college girl, "I found myself very concerned with what others thought of me. I wanted every person to think highly of me, so I would constantly change the way I acted, depending upon the people I was with." When this girl listened, she was listening with a desire to be what she thought the other person wanted her to be instead of her real self.

Guys do this too. "Being a normal Christian boy," writes Lanny, "I am quite concerned when it comes to matters with the opposite sex. I have had some problems in these matters because I have trouble opening up and just doing what I really think I should do. So many of my actions and most of everything I say on a date are 'censored' to make a certain impression on the girl. I would really like to be able to open up and be myself rather than building an image for a girl. I find being honest with others is very hard for me."

So many of us *use* listening to find out what others want, and then try to make ourselves fit the pattern we discover. We put on a mask and hide our true feelings.

The trouble is, putting on a mask pushes the *real* you further and further from others. Instead of getting closer, you withdraw. The result of this way of trying to relate to others, according to Sociologist Moris Rosenberg, is a kind of independence and "a haunting sense of isolation and loneliness."[2] Far too many of my young friends express just this kind of feeling!

"Throughout high school," says a guy from New Jersey, "I realized that I really had no one I could call a best friend. I had many acquaintances, but no really close friendships. Even in church I always seemed to be the third wheel on the bicycle. I feel like I have missed something by not having close friends."

It really does hurt, this being cut off from others. "I can't explain," says another guy. "Many people are close to me, but I am always a 'loner' inside. I always give 100 percent, but I never reveal my inside."

This is one of the biggest, if not *the* biggest, limitation on listening. Listening, even with the right motives, can only get a person so far in a relationship. The only thing that can get you further is talking—talking to "reveal my inside."

"Don't be afraid to reveal yourself to others," says a Wheaton College girl. "This way you find out about yourself, and make the other person want to reveal himself." This isn't easy, of course. One guy calls it a "risk" but insists that we must learn to "take the risk in sharing with someone, so that a close friendship can develop. For example, if you share a personal experience or feeling for the first few times there is always a nagging fear of overexposing yourself to criticism, and not having the other person respond favorably."

That fear is always there in relationships. But it's important to remember that the fear is there for the other guy too!

Why stress this?

Because just as you're wondering how the other person is reacting to you, *he's* wondering, *What does he think of me now?* And there is only one way for a person to find out what is going on inside another. That person has to tell him. The Bible points this out when it says, "No one can really know what anyone else is thinking, or what he is really like, except that person himself" (1 Cor. 2:11) So we *have* to open up and to reveal ourselves to each other if anyone is to know us. We have to open up to draw closer, no matter how well we listen.

Actually, listening without revealing ourselves in return will make others feel uneasy. If they share with us and we're unwilling to share in return, it's likely to make them suspicious of us and our motives. We all know people who try to use us, e.g., for status ("He must have something because the most popular girls date him."), for a prop ("If I didn't have someone to tell all my troubles to I'd just *die!*"), to give us a feeling of power ("Oh, he always does what I want to do."), or in other ways. In fact, one psychiatrist believes that "whenever two people meet, the strong personality, after an initial period of psychic probing, knowingly or otherwise tries to coerce the weaker one by attempting to become the dominant leader."[3] We may not think this is right, but we know that this kind of thing happens all the time. Others know it too. And when we aren't willing to reveal our true selves, it's not surprising that others misunderstand our motives.

Dependence

There's probably no more significant relationship word

than *dependence,* particularly when it's preceded by some of its prefixes.

By itself, dependence reflects the kind of relationship that's right for a small child to have with his parents. A child depends on his parents to meet his physical needs, to supply emotional support, and to make important decisions for him. Some people never get over this childhood way of relating to others. They want someone to lean on, someone to make decisions for them, someone to be strong for them.

The other side of this dependency relationship is called counterdependency. It pictures a person who *wants* to have others depend on *him.* For parents of small children this is fine. But when the person you want to lean on you is another teenager or a young adult, the attitude is unhealthy. It's unhealthy because you're trying to *use* this person to satisfy your need to feel strong. And this keeps him from growing up.

I used to think the goal of growing up was to become independent—to get to the place where I didn't need to rely on others, and where I could stand alone. The trouble is, I've discovered that I still really can't stand alone. I need others—my students (who are my friends), my wife, my children, other adults. And I've discovered that the Bible comes on strong in saying that Christians need each other to develop spiritually. We just can't be independent. Even the apostle Paul, who had a lot more going for him than either you or I have, wrote to the Romans, "I long to visit you so that I can impart to you the faith that will help your church grow strong in the Lord." And then he quickly added, "Then, too, I need your help, for I want not only to share my faith with you but be encouraged by yours: each of us will be a blessing to the other" (Rom. 1:11–12).

So the goal isn't becoming independent of others. It's becoming *interdependent with* others that "each of us" may be "a blessing to the other."

The crucial thing about interdependence is that it can never happen in a relationship where one always gives and the other always receives. It's a relationship where each gives and each receives. This is why just listening (which is receiving) can never lead to the kind of closeness with others we want and need. And this is why the kids who advised "open up to others" were zeroing in on one of the biggest of all factors in building relationships.

Ted, from Illinois, writes, "If you as a person are not willing to give part of yourself, or open up to a person, a person will not open up to you." But what happens when we seem to be open, and others draw back? Remember Carl, whose story opened this book? This was how he felt. Yet, as I spoke more with him, it became clear that he misunderstood what opening up involves, and that his misunderstanding was at the root of his relationship problem. Let's look at what he said again, and ask, What does opening up seem to mean to Carl? Here's what he said:

> Whenever people get to know me, they pull away from me. Like one girl I knew in high school. We went out a few times, and we got along pretty well. Then I began to tell her what I thought about things, and to tell her my ideas. And, well, she just seemed to close up and pull away.

Reading it over, it's clear that Carl thought of people as getting to know him when he told them "what I thought about things" and when he shared his "ideas." But he was wrong. He told what he thought, but he told very little about *himself*.

Look at this quote from a college girl and note the difference between her idea of sharing and Carl's: "I have to share things with someone," Helen writes, "or I'll burst. And I have to share everything, especially the deepest thoughts and impressions. I can't share these things with Sue or John Doe over the dining hall table; it has to be with somebody I really trust and respect. Therefore, I find a real need for *deep,* close relationships—with friends, and with God."

See it? To Helen sharing means telling someone your "deepest thoughts and impressions." It means getting down to the "feeling" level of life. To Carl, it meant telling another person his thoughts and ideas on various issues.

There's a world of difference between these two kinds of openness. When other people listen to us telling our ideas, they have no sense of drawing close to us as a person. But when we share our feelings and thoughts and impressions they understand that we are inviting them into our lives. They sense our attempt to draw closer to them as persons.

Not everyone will accept this kind of invitation. And we don't want to extend it to everyone we meet. It's quite all right to operate on an acquaintance level with most people. But with some we want and need a deeper friendship. We want an interdependent relationship in which both of us give and both of us receive.

To reach out toward this kind of relationship we simply have to express our willingness to draw closer to others. We have to listen with concern, and we have to open up to share something of ourselves.

Opening the door

There are a number of ways to open the door to deeper personal relationships—ways that we can listen and respond that will tell others when we are willing to come closer. What are some of them?

Concentrate on listening. Often we don't truly listen to others. You've seen people taking part in conversations like this. One person is talking, but no one else is listening. Everyone is just waiting for that person to stop talking so he can start in!

At times like these we're usually thinking more about what we plan to say next than about what the other person is saying. Our eyes wander, we open our mouth at the slightest pause in the other person's stream of words, we seem agi-

tated and eager to have our turn to speak.

No, listening that says "I'm interested and willing to come closer" is the kind of listening that communicates caring. It's not worrying about what I plan to say next, but trying honestly to understand what the other person is saying now. I may not understand. I may miss the point. But if I'm really trying to understand, that other person will sense it and will recognize the fact that I'm holding open the door of friendship.

Listen for feelings. Carl's problem was that he felt free to share his ideas but not his feelings. Most of us do this to some extent. And when we have feelings to share, we often translate them up into ideas.

It's like this: I may feel very much afraid to show my true self to another person. But rather than saying this right out, I'd probably say something like this: "I think everyone has a right to some privacy." Or, "It's dangerous to tell another person too much about yourself, don't you think?" I may be unhappy just now about a rift with my teenage son; but instead of stating my feelings, I might say, "Teens today just don't appreciate their parents."

Usually when we try to express feelings as thoughts we give many clues to what we're really trying to say. Uncertain looks. Hesitation when we talk. Angrily blurting out a statement. Flippancy. All these tell that feelings are flowing with our words and our thoughts.

If we listen, we can begin to hear some of the feelings. When we listen for feelings, we get a better idea of what a person is really trying to communicate. For instance, Carol was one high schooler who responded to a question I asked about her friendships. Carol uses words here that express ideas, but everything she says indicates that underneath are some very deep and important feelings. If she said these words to you, what feelings might you think she was trying to share?

> It seems that I have a lot of friends, but hardly any real or close ones. They are nice but at times distant or spiteful, or they are nice to me but talk about me. Even the kids I consider to be close friends at times seem to look down on me.

The feelings come out, don't they?

And when we listen for them, we hear them.

Of course, we may misunderstand the feelings we think we hear. Then our listening can lead to *reflecting,* to throwing back what we think we've heard for our friend to check out for us. A reflecting response to Carol that says I want to understand what she's saying might be, "You feel uncertain about how your friends feel about you?" Or, "You don't feel you can trust your friends, then?" Responses like these show that we're trying to understand what is really important to the other person; that we don't care about abstract ideas, but about *her.* And that we care enough to be sensitive to how she feels.

This, like listening carefully, can be an expression of true concern. It can show another person that the door is open if he wants to come closer.

Respond with self-revelation. I said earlier that our goal in personal relationships should be to move toward *interdependence,* not independence or some form of dependency. This kind of relationship means that we must give as well as receive. This is where self-revelation fits in.

When we respond to another person by revealing something of ourselves—right down on that "feeling" level where we live—we tell them that we're willing to give. "Sincere listening can do a great deal to improve relationships," says a collegian. "Have a sympathetic and understanding ear—and be honest in your responses. But," he goes on, "be willing to give of your innermost self—don't make them do all the giving."

Often we're hesitant about revealing ourselves. We feel that others won't accept or like us if they find out what we're really like. But even the apostle Paul didn't hide things about himself that others might have criticized. In one place he wrote in this very revealing way to a group of people who were rebelling against his leadership:

> I think you ought to know, dear brothers, about the hard time we went through in Asia. We were really crushed and overwhelmed and feared we would never live through it. We felt we were doomed to die and saw how powerless we were to help ourselves (2 Cor. 1:8–9).

Today we tend to think that a dedicated Christian (especially a leader!) shouldn't ever feel "down," and that if he does he certainly shouldn't let others discover it. But that wasn't Paul's way of living with others, and it's not God's way for us. Paul understood that if we are to be close to others we have to be honest with them. And that revealing our real selves—our real feelings and experiences and thoughts and needs, and even our failings—is the only way to become truly close and interdependent.

In practice, when we show our real selves to others they sometimes do draw back. Some aren't ready for a close relationship just yet. Others may not want a close relationship with us. When someone draws back after we reveal ourselves to him a time or two, this is a sign that our invitation to closeness has been rejected for now. And that's all right. We don't want to force ourselves on others. We simply want to invite them—when they're ready and when they want to—to draw closer to us. As an invitation, there's nothing so unmistakable as sharing something, revealing something, of our real selves.

How does a person accept our invitation to closeness? By revealing more of himself. Not *all* of himself. Not at first, certainly. But more than before. And so we begin a give-and-take relationship—a friendship that over a period of time can become deeper and closer.

While we shouldn't push ourselves on others by revealing too much too fast (a course that's likely to frighten most people away!), we should remember that some sharing of ourselves marks our willingness to develop a meaningful friendship. Others may be eagerly waiting for some sign from us that they are welcome in our lives.

Follow up with warmth. I add this almost as an afterthought. Usually, after you've had a time of sharing with another person on a deeper level, you begin to wonder afterward, *Did I tell him too much? How does he feel about me now? Is he sorry now he told me as much as he did?* This is only natural, and the other person probably has the same questions.

So it's good to reassure him the next time you see him. I don't mean that you should make a big thing of it. Just a friendly smile or a wave across the campus is enough. Some sign that you're glad, really glad, to see him.

Warmth, expressed in these or other ways, says what is very important for us to say: "I'm not sorry we came closer. You are still important to me, and the door is still open. I'm willing to listen and to share with you again."

Steps to take

1. Here are some terms the author feels are very important to understand in thinking about personal relationships. Jot down your understanding of each, and then check them out in this chapter.

listening
reflecting
interdependence
self-revealing

2. The "opening the door" section of this chapter gives several suggestions for improving relationships with others. Try one or two of them on a person with whom you want to develop a closer friendship.

3 At ease

Barb, a twenty-one-year-old from Indiana, makes a penetrating comment: "Usually young people need more confidence and assurance that they are worthy human beings. In a group of Christian friends, emphasis should be on acceptance of others; when one is accepted he is much more likely to give of himself, knowing that he won't be snubbed.

Knowing you're accepted, feeling like a worthy human being, and feeling good about yourself, are vital to finding freedom to open up with others. All the "how to" suggestions in the world won't help unless you can honestly accept and love yourself, and so find the freedom to be at ease.

"One of the hardest things in life," writes a nineteen-year-old, "is finding your own unique personality among your social group, which is our situation in the school. I have problems because I tend to rely on others for identity. I feel a compulsion to conform to things that will make me an 'in' kid. I find myself reacting in certain ways because I know that the general reaction of others will be favorable. I want to be myself. But what am I? What can I as a unique person contribute?"

This is a pretty common response to someone who says, as kids did in the last chapter, "Just be yourself and reveal yourself honestly to others." Most of us would like to, but it's taking a pretty big risk. We feel that "compulsion to conform," to say and to do things to make others respond favorably to us.

After living like this for a while, sort of performing while someone else writes the script, we may very well wonder what the real "me" is like!

Then, too, a lot of us are uncertain (or even unhappy) about what we think of as our real selves. Such dissatisfaction with ourselves is probably behind many of the statements kids made—statements that sounded something like this: "I have received much advice on how to fit in with others. But I have always been too introverted to use it." And this: "I found it hard to relate to the others because I knew no Christians at school, because they were so different (personality-wise) from me, and because I was still very self-conscious."

When we feel self-conscious and uncertain about ourselves, it's hard to do what one college student suggests: just "be natural, don't put up a front."

Easy to say, isn't it? But terrifically hard to do.

Yet, even the Bible indicates we needn't take our failings as seriously as we sometimes do. "Let everyone be sure that he is doing his very best," it says in Galatians, "for then he will have the personal satisfaction of work well-done, and won't need to compare himself with someone else. Each of us must bear some faults and burdens of his own. For none of us is perfect!" (Gal. 6:4–5). So we really *are* to accept ourselves, with all our limitations, and just try to be ourselves—not someone else.

We're to do our very best, and forget about comparisons with others that make us wish we were different or better.

Faults, or sins?

Something that seems to bother Christians a lot is differentiating between faults and sins. What others might feel free to dismiss as a fault, a Christian is likely to classify as a sin.

For instance, a common problem that Becky points up might be taken either way by different people. "I would say," Becky writes, "that none of us really has enough genuine love for one another. We don't really care what happens to the other person, what his problems are, etc. Because of this, it's hard to really relate to others." Now, this is clearly a good point—a true evaluation. We *don't* have enough love. If we did truly care about others, it would transform our personal relationships.

But is this a fault (that is, should we look at this just as a problem to be solved), or is it a sin (that is, should we look at it as a *wrong,* concerning which we ought to feel guilty)?

The Christian is apt to view this first of all as a sin, and begin to feel guilty when he becomes aware of his lack of love. He remembers some things the Bible says about loving others: "Most important of all, continue to show deep love for each other" (1 Peter 4:8). And, "For the whole Law can be summed up in this one command: 'Love others as you love yourself' " (Gal. 5:14). Discovering our lack of love and comparing ourselves to these standards, it's easy to feel very guilty and unhappy about ourselves.

Then we fall into a terribly easy and horribly deceiving way of looking at that real *me* that we're asked to reveal in personal relationships.

It goes something like this:

"I know I ought to love others. But I don't. Why don't I? I guess I'm just a failure as a Christian. I'm really no good at all." And who would be willing to reveal a self that's no good?

Strangely, in feeling this way about ourselves we break the other half of the commandment we were worried about!

Remember how Jesus first stated it? A lawyer had asked Him a question:

> "Sir, which is the most important command in the laws of Moses?"
>
> Jesus replied, " 'Love the Lord your God with all your heart, soul and mind.' That is the first and greatest commandment. The second most important is similar, 'Love your neighbor as much as you love yourself' " (Matt. 22:36–39).

Notice what Christ is saying in this command to love others. He's giving equal weight to the command to *love ourselves!* And we are to love ourselves just as thoroughly and unselfishly as we are supposed to love others.

Now, whatever else we can say about love, we know that it doesn't hate or reject its object. It doesn't condemn or push away; it doesn't feel *repelled by.* So when we fail to like ourselves and to accept ourselves, we've wandered a long way off God's track. This simply is not the way God wants us to feel.

Many of my correspondents seem to understand this very clearly. "Accept yourself and move in with other people, not worrying so much what they think," said one teen.

Another writes, "I would say: Believe that you are an important person—the person who has self-worth believes that others are important. Don't worry about what others think of you so much that you can't be yourself. Get right with God . . . then you never have to be embarrassed about what you do, regardless of what other people's reaction to you is."

Perhaps one guy summed it all up in these words: "A person must feel accepted by God and *free* to be the kind of person God will use."

This may seem like a pretty big order. But if we understand who we really are, we'll be well on our way.

Accepted and free

It's hard to feel accepted and free in a relationship that calls for a certain level of performance on our part. And most relationships we've had with others seem to do just

this. An employee has to perform his job well if he expects to stay on good terms with his boss. If someone does you a favor, you feel obligated to pay him back. And when you do something to displease another, you usually feel you have to do something to get back on his good side. Like bringing flowers to your girl after a fight. Or apologizing to Dad when you keep the car longer than you were supposed to.

In all these ways we try to balance our social debts to others to make sure they will accept and like us.

But what happens when we haven't performed as we should? And when we don't know how to make amends? For one thing, we probably don't feel confident in that relationship. We're apt to cringe inside—at least a little bit—when we meet.

When that person is important to us, and when we respect his opinion of us, there's a second impact of our failure to perform. We feel the other person doesn't accept us, and we find it hard to accept ourselves! We feel guilty. Unimportant. Unworthy.

At times like these we don't even like ourselves.

All this is a direct result of building relationships on a pay-as-you-go basis: All this results from the feeling that you have to live up to certain standards, to perform up to others' expectations in order to be accepted.

So one of the most important questions we can ask about personal relationships, and about ourselves, is this: Is a person to be valued on the basis of his performance? Do my actions make me important—intrinsically worthwhile? Or is it something else?

And here the Christian gospel has a unique and very special answer. It starts off by recognizing an obvious fact: If we measure ourselves by our performance, everyone fails. As far as doing right and being truly good are concerned, we all fall short—very short. Do we love others? Have enough concern for them? Never! Not by God's standards. Not even by our own.

So if our attitude toward ourselves is to be based on how well we live up to what is good and right (especially if we accept the Bible's high standards of right), we're bound to feel bad about ourselves. We're bound to feel guilty and unworthy, because we are.

Here the gospel takes a surprising twist. For the gospel says that we are not to build our personal relationships (with God, with ourselves, or with others) on performance. *We are to forget all about performance.*

Our performance has nothing to do with our value, or with our personal relationships. God has invented a new way.

We can most clearly see this new way of relating when we look at how God wants us to relate to Him. That way is seen in this fascinating New Testament passage:

> For whatever God says to us is full of living power: it is sharper than the sharpest dagger, cutting swift and deep into our innermost thoughts and desires with all their parts, exposing us for what we really are.
>
> He knows about everyone, everywhere. Everything about us is bare and wide open to the all-seeing eyes of our living God; nothing can be hidden from him to whom we must explain all that we have done (Heb. 4:12-13).

See the picture here? God has *complete* knowledge of us. We can't hide anything from Him. Our whole life, our innermost thoughts and desires, are "bare and wide open" to Him, so that He knows us "for what we really are."

Yet, knowing all this, knowing every failure and every sin that might make us feel guilt and cringe in His presence, God has a peculiar attitude toward us, and He wants us to feel an amazing freedom with Him.

> But Jesus the Son of God is our great High Priest who has gone to heaven itself to help us; therefore let us never stop trusting him. This High Priest of ours understands our weaknesses, since he had the same temptations we do, though he never once gave way to them and sinned. So let us come boldly to the very throne of God and stay there to receive his mercy and to find grace to help us in our times of need (Heb. 4:14–16).

Far then from being repelled by our real selves, God accepts us and welcomes us as we are! He even invites us to come to Him *boldly*—not cringing—to "the very throne of God."

We know that there we can find mercy for our weaknesses and failures. And grace, to help us to a new way of life.

Somehow God has put our relationship with Him on a basis that is completely different from performance. When it comes to thinking about ourselves as persons, we need to forget our actions—and our sins—if we're to find the freedom to love ourselves and to love others.

I suppose it's strange for a writer of a Christian book to advise you to forget about sin in thinking about yourself, and your relationship with God. But that's just what I have to say. That's what the Bible says. That's what the gospel is all about.

The power of forgiveness

I feel real frustration because I know that some will misunderstand what I'm saying—no matter how I say it. "Forget about sin" will come as a jolting shock. "How horrible," they'll say. "Why, the Bible talks so much about sin. The Bible says we're all sinners, and that our guilt and our doubt about ourselves aren't just psychological—they're rooted in the very realities of human existence. We can only understand ourselves," these people will say, "if we remember that we're sinners and live in fear of the power of sin all our lives. Forget about sin? Heresy!"

I can understand the reaction. We do need to understand ourselves as sinners. At first. If we didn't, we might think we could get along with God the same way we try to get along with people. By performing. By doing something good. If we should do wrong, we try somehow to make up for it by putting an extra dollar in the collection plate, or reading the Bible for an hour, or promising never to do again whatever we did wrong.

The Bible calls this a "good works" approach to relationship but makes it clear that trying to be "good enough to gain God's favor" simply "is not God's way of salvation" (Rom. 10:3).

But once we've recognized the futility of trying to get on good terms with God by what we do, we're supposed to forget about sin and start focusing on *forgiveness*.

The Bible has a lot of things to say about forgiveness. Things so important that a few passages on the subject ought to be quoted—just to help you see I'm not really off the track with all this "forget sin" advice. Look these Bible portions over and see what you think they're saying. What seems particularly important to me is italicized.

Talking about Abraham, the Bible says,

> For the Scriptures tell us Abraham believed God, and that is why *God canceled his sins and declared him 'not guilty.'* But didn't he earn his right to heaven by all the good things he did? No, *for being saved is a gift;* if a person could earn it by being good, then it wouldn't be free—but it is! It is *given* to those who do *not* work for it. For God *declares sinners to be good in His sight* if they have faith in

Christ to save them from God's wrath.

King David spoke of this, describing the happiness of an *undeserving sinner who is declared 'not guilty' by God.* "Blessed, and to be envied," he said, "are those *whose sins are forgiven and put out of sight.* Yes, what joy there is for anyone whose *sins are no longer counted against him*" (Rom. 4:3–8).

Other passages talk the same way about sins being forgiven and put out of sight, and no longer counted. "*God declares we are 'not guilty' of offending him* if we trust in Jesus Christ," Romans 3:24 says, and calls Jesus the one who "*freely takes away our sins.*" In the Old Testament, God promises to relate to us in a new way in Christ, "and then he adds, 'I will *never again remember their sins and lawless deeds.*' Now, when sins have once been *forever forgiven and forgotten,* there is *no need to offer more sacrifices to get rid of them*" (Heb. 10:17–18).

Yes, we can forget about our sins when we come to trust Jesus Christ, *because God has.* Somehow the death of Christ on the cross for sin canceled out sins perfectly. It canceled them out so perfectly that our sins are no longer even an issue. God forgives us. He declares us to be good. Our sins are put out of His sight.

So we *know* God's attitude toward us. He loves us. He likes us. He accepts us. To Him we're always welcome, because we *are* "just and good." "God showed His great love for us by sending Christ to die for us while we were sinners," the Bible says. And it goes on:

> Since by his blood he did all this for us as sinners, how much more will he do for us *now that He has declared us not guilty?* Now he will save us from all of God's wrath to come. And since, when we were his enemies we were brought back to God by the death of his Son, what *blessings he must have for us now that we are his friends,* and he is living within us! (Rom. 5:9–10).

The power of forgiveness, turned loose in the death of Christ on the cross, frees us to feel good and happy about ourselves. It frees us to be ourselves with God, and to accept ourselves in God's sight, with full assurance that we are so very well loved by Him.

We are sure of forgiveness, for we have been forgiven. We are accepted, declared not guilty by God. Accepted, and free.

Patterns

Why have I spent so much time developing the theme of relationship with God? Because it seems to me that there are only two basic patterns on which personal relationship can be established. One of them is a performance pattern, where I *do* something to earn acceptance. The other is a love pattern, where I am fully and freely accepted as I am, with forgiveness overcoming all my failures and my lacks.

These two patterns are most perfectly modeled in our relationship with God. How many of us have struggled to feel good enough to be His friend, only to discover that we never live up to our own standards, much less His? How many of us have felt the guilt this produces? How many then have either gone through the motions of pretending to be right with God, or have given up on God altogether? No, the only thing that seeking a relationship with God on a works basis can ever do is to cut us off from Him. For the guiltier we feel, the less freedom we have to be honest with Him. We know that on the basis of what we do we simply haven't earned His acceptance.

How freeing the gospel message is when we grasp the fact that God offers us a different kind of relationship. He loves, He accepts, He forgives us freely in Christ. He knows us as we are, and accepts us anyway.

This model of a relationship founded on forgiving love is one we have to learn to apply in our relationship with ourselves, and with others. When we learn to accept love and to give love, our whole lives are changed—in a variety of ways.

Forgiveness frees us to accept ourselves. Earlier in the chapter Barb said, "Usually young people need more confidence and assurance that they are worthy human beings." And this is exactly right. We all need to know that we are intrinsically worthwhile. We need to feel that if we let go and be our real selves, we'll like the person who emerges.

This is one reason why the Bible insists we are to love others and to love ourselves. Because people are worth loving.

We must not become so caught up thinking of people as sinners that we forget that, according to God, man is made in His own image. And that image has persisted even after sin became part of the human personality (cf. Gen. 9:6). In God's image, as true persons, God made us with a capacity like His own to *love* and to *choose* and to *do*.

The unique person that *you* are has all this tremendous potential. As a Christian, you have even more. "God has given each of you," the Bible says to believers, "some special abilities" which you are "to use . . . to help each other, passing on to others God's many kinds of blessings" (1 Peter 4:10).

Worthy? Valuable? Tremendously!

If you let go and become your real self, this "like God" personality can and will emerge.

You aren't like this now, I know. Neither am I. The real me, the "like God" me that God renewed when I trusted

Christ, is often blocked by my wrong desires, wrong decisions, and wrong actions. But I don't have to hide this from myself, or work hard to make up for my failings. Instead, I am to pattern my feelings about myself on the model given in Christ. I am to forgive. I am to love—myself.

Have you forgiven yourself?

Have you learned to love yourself?

I hope so. It's God's way. And it brings us freedom.

Forgiveness frees us to be ourselves. Having the ability to love and to forgive ourselves, we find a new freedom with others. We feel less pressure to put up a front and to act in ways designed to earn acceptance. One guy whom I quoted earlier expressed this kind of freedom when he wrote, 'Be natural—don't put up a front. Everyone has faults. The people who will accept you with your faults will be your true friends."

Can you sense the freedom he feels?

This is a hard freedom to find. We tend to relive experiences—especially the ones where we've goofed something up. "Oh, why did I ever say *that!*" torments many of us. Just as often we go over things we might have said but didn't. We can't seem to forget them.

If you've reacted like this, the idea of "be natural" is really threatening. You're constantly on guard against some tormenting mistake. So you stiffen up, pull back. No wonder it's so hard to be yourself.

"Be yourself," says a college girl. "Don't worry about making an example or impression. People (especially other kids) see through a facade. You'll feel a lot more at ease and find it easier to relate to people."

When we've learned to forgive ourselves, we're able to break out into the open. We can risk making mistakes because we know we don't need to torment ourselves over them. Our worth—even to ourselves—doesn't depend on our performance. We can afford to forgive, and forget.

Coming out into the open like this, reassured by self-love and self-forgiveness, we do "feel more at ease and find it easier to relate to people."

Forgiveness does free us to be ourselves.

Forgiveness releases transforming power. This is the last thing to remember. I imagine someone who reads this book will be worried that I am telling you to just go out and sin as much as you want, and forget about it. Not at all. Because that isn't the way forgiveness works.

The Bible tells us, "Just think how much more surely the blood of Christ [the source of our forgiveness] will transform our lives and hearts. His sacrifice frees us from the worry of having to obey the old rules and makes us want to serve the living God" (Heb. 9:14).

Earlier I asked, Are we to look at lack of love as a problem to be solved, or as a wrong concerning which to feel guilty? Here's the answer: We are *not* to look at it as a wrong. As a wrong, a sin, it has been forgiven.

But it is a problem—an area in which we need to experience God's power to "transform our lives and hearts . . . making us want to serve the living God." Freed by forgiveness to recognize and accept our problems, we are perfectly free to approach God and seek His grace to help in these times of our need.

Shirley pictures what I mean as she describes her way of life: "The way I've found that works is to say, 'God, You see how I just don't relate well with that group and I know You want me to be free and open with people. So please, Lord, help!' So God, in His great way of handling things, slowly starts presenting me with situations where I have the opportunity to relate. Then, when I blow my big chance and walk away muttering, He very kindly starts over again until I finally get it—I can actually fit in."

Freed from worry, and freed to trust God to transform us, we can afford to live at ease. This is God's great way.

Steps to take

1. How would you describe your present relationship with God?
   a. strained
   b. distant
   c. uncertain
   d. relaxed but reverent

   From what the author said in this chapter, what do you think might be the cause of each kind of relationship?

2. If you'd like a more confident relationship with God, read over pages 41 through 45, studying especially the biblical passages quoted. Can you tell God now that you accept His forgiveness?

3. The author has said that it's important for us to accept and forgive ourselves if we're to find freedom in relating to others. Can you recall *why* this is true?

4 Becoming

The things you've read in the last chapter probably have left you with a lot of questions. Perhaps some of them are like the questions that plague this sixteen-year-old Montana girl. "I would ask," she writes, "how can I stop being so self-conscious about whether I will be accepted, how I am impressing others, whether I am 'popular'? How can I stop comparing my popularity with that of others who are even shyer than I am, just to boost my own ego? How can I be well liked since I am not outgoing or talkative except to close friends? I don't know what I'm doing wrong, or how to correct it."

This girl doesn't *want* to "accept herself as is." She wants to change!

It would be tragic to see forgiving love as simply comforting. It's far more. It unlocks our potential to change.

When we think about it, we can understand why. The Bible describes what happens when we begin to take forgiveness seriously—and when we fail to. "If we say that we have no sin," it says, "we are only fooling ourselves,

and refusing to accept the truth. But if we confess our sins to him, he can be depended on to forgive us and to cleanse us from every wrong. And it is perfectly proper for God to do this for us because Christ died to wash away our sins" (1 John 1:8–9).

Refusing to accept the truth and to seek forgiveness closes the door to change. Realizing the freedom cleansing brings opens us to change—and motivates us.

Just now I got up from the typewriter and went out into the living room where my two boys were arguing. My youngest, in an angry voice, was doggedly defending his right to bicker and his innocence in a sock-throwing incident. (Both my guys—and me too!—love to roll pairs of socks into balls and fire them at empty boxes, and at each other.) At seven Timmy hasn't yet learned to admit his fault, or to accept forgiving love. Instead, he defends himself, pretending even to himself that *he* isn't at fault. The result is only anger—anger at himself and anger that strikes out to blame others.

When Tim is feeling like this, he's unreachable. And he is unable to change. All his energy is focused on fighting to justify himself. In putting up walls to protect and hide himself, he cuts off the possibility of change.

It's like this with all of us. When we can't accept our failings and our faults, or experience the cleansing that forgiveness brings, our personalities become static. We find ourselves in bondage to all we hate in ourselves and in others.

So seeing ourselves as we are, and accepting ourselves as persons who live in need of cleansing, is really the first step in becoming new persons.

It is at this point that coming to understand the fantastic fullness of God's forgiveness frees us. For God does accept us as we are—without recrimination and without penalty (for Christ has taken our penalty). If we can really see God as eager to embrace us when we come to Him as we are, the defensive walls that keep us static and immobile dissolve.

One of the warmest stories Jesus told helps us to *feel* the warmth and power of this kind of forgiveness. The father in the story acts and feels as God does; the son acts and feels as we have acted and as we can act. Here's the story. Read it over again and see if you can feel with both the father and the young man as you react to the questions in the margin.

A man had two sons. When the younger told his father, "I want my share of your estate now, instead of waiting until you die!" his father agreed to divide his wealth between his sons.

How did the father feel on this rejection by his son?

A few days later this younger son packed all his belongings and took a trip to a distant land, and there wasted all his money on parties and prostitutes. About the time his money was gone, a great famine swept over the land, and he began to starve. He persuaded a local farmer to hire him to feed pigs. The boy became so hungry that even the pods he was feeding the swine looked good to him. And no one gave him anything.

How much fun do you think it is to go your own way apart from God?

When he finally came to his senses, he said to himself, "At home even the hired men have food enough and to spare, and here I am, dying of hunger! I will go home to my father and say, 'Father, I have sinned against both heaven and you, and am no longer worthy of being called your son. Please take me on as a hired man.' "

Was deciding to confess his sin easy? Or the decision to go to his father?

So he returned home to his father. And while he was still a long distance away, his father saw him coming and was filled with loving pity and ran and embraced him and kissed him. His son said to him, "Father, I have sinned against heaven and you, and am not worthy to be called your son—"

Did the father sit back and wait for the son to crawl?

But the father said to the slaves, "Quick! Bring the finest robe in the house and put it on him. And a jeweled ring for his finger; and shoes! And kill the calf we have in the fattening pen. We must celebrate with a feast, for this son of mine was dead and has returned to life! He was lost and is found!" So the party began (Lk 15:11–24).

How was the boy treated? As a returned son? As a slave? As a "son in disgrace"?

Knowing we are loved just like this can break down the barriers that keep *us* from change. Suddenly, instead of having to strike out and defend ourselves, we can *be* ourselves. As we really are. And know that we are completely loved and completely accepted.

Bruce Larson describes how this happens in his own life, and how he is freed to *become* by experiencing forgiving love:

> Christ loves us *just as we are.* We are impatient, grumpy, irritable, nagging, fault-finding at home or in the office or in school because we really hate ourselves. It is difficult to believe that right now, in the light of what we have just done, God loves us as much as He says He does. When I find myself critical of the people I live with at home or work, I don't need more patience but time alone to let God remind me of His love for me. When I know that I am loved by Him and am forgiven for present failures, then I find the things that have been so irritating in my family members or colleagues become trivial. We must learn to take the Cross seriously and experience day by day and moment by moment Christ's overpowering love and forgiveness, not only for sins past, but for sins present. He does not say to us, "Change, that I might love you." As we read the biblical record of Jesus talking with people, we sense His total love for them as they are. This love motivates them to change.[1]

More than motivation

Actually, the personality transformation that Christianity promises rests on more than pumping up our own motivation.

It is true that love is motivating and forgiveness is freeing—for everyone, Christian and non-Christian alike. Why not? God made persons this way. The principles demonstrated in the gospel are the very principles that fit the human personality He invented. But accepting God's forgiveness in Christ goes far beyond the psychological. The Bible tells us that when we trust Christ for forgiveness, God releases a far more potent and dynamic force in us.

Many of the kids who wrote me referred in various ways to this dynamic. "I think that it is essential to accept others with an open mind, realizing that not everyone is going to think and act like you. Yet to do this successfully takes a great deal of love which always comes from yourself but can be gotten from God."

Another collegian says the same thing this way: "Pray to God that He'll give you a real love and interest in the individual and who he really is." Somehow, these young people feel, God Himself has become a source of our power to change.

And that is what the Bible says. "You have a new life," it reports in one place. "It was not passed on to you from your parents, for the life they gave you will fade away. This new one will last forever, for it comes from Christ" (1 Peter 1:23). This new life from Christ wells up in us, overflowing and replacing the old life and the old ways. "Now you can have real love for everyone because your souls have been cleansed from selfishness and hatred when you trusted Christ to save you" (1 Peter 1:22).

Talking about the same thing in a little different way, the Bible calls this new life Christianity's great secret:

"Christ in you, the hope of glory" (Col. 1:27 AV).

Now, none of this is "theological jargon." It's all very practical and very real. And what it boils down to is this: With forgiveness, God Himself enters our lives and makes basic, down-underneath changes in our personalities. Before becoming Christians, sin (God's word for that rebellious kink in our personalities that keeps us from becoming the truly good persons we'd like to be) cut us off from "becoming." Sin limited the changes we could make in our lives. But God coming into our lives *takes that limit off!* He opens up the future to us, freeing us to make the most basic changes in the way we think and feel and in the ways we relate to others. He makes it possible for us to become the free, loving and being loved persons we want to be.

Often we miss the central fact that relating to others hinges on what we are, and little else. One college man explained why he has trouble fitting in with others at his school: "I have found that I have trouble relating to non-Christians basically because of my vocabulary. I've gone to a fundamental church all my life and have been indoctrinated with the 'proper evangelical vernacular.' The language of the King James Version doesn't break down the barriers between the Christian and the non-Christian."

Now, I'm sorry, but this is *not* the basic reason he doesn't relate. It's just an excuse, a cop-out. When we don't relate to others it's not our *vocabularies*—it's our *personalities!* "Language" doesn't break down barriers—love does! This guy is kidding himself; and if you've made similar excuses, you're kidding yourself too. Your problem is that you need to become the kind of person who is truly good and loving. What keeps you—and all of us—away from others is our failure to become the kind of persons we need to be to relate to them.

You need to *become.*

So far, then, I've suggested that becoming a new and different kind of person—the person you really want to be—depends on two things. First, on understanding and accepting the forgiving love of God in Christ. Second, on the new, unlimited life that God Himself plants in your personality when you do accept His forgiveness. Christ's power within takes your limitations off, and makes it possible for you to become the kind of person who can relate in warmth and love to others. So the potential for change is there—inside.

This is important. As a Christian you *have* the potential to become. There is nothing you need to do, or can do, to get it. You don't even need to pray for it. You've already got it. The potential is there.

So the only thing left for us to do is to live it out, to actually become.

No wonder the Bible freely issues instructions like this: "Follow God's example in everything you do just as a much loved child imitates his father" (Eph. 5:1). We can do it! And "throw off your old evil nature [that rebellious way of life that sin produces]. . . . Now your attitudes and thoughts must all be constantly changing for the better. Yes, you must be a new and different person, holy and good. Clothe yourself with this new nature" (Eph. 4:22–24).

We can do this! Since we have God's new life within, we need only to let it out. We need only to become.

How?

There's a lot behind the *how* to grow and develop as a Christian that I'm about to suggest. But it isn't the purpose of this book to explore a lot of it. I've written about much of it in earlier *Answers for Youth* books, particularly the last chapters of *How I Can Be Real* and *How I Can Experience God.* So I feel free to focus on one aspect of "becoming" that we often overlook. It's stated in a quote we just read: "Follow God's example in everything you do just as a much loved child imitates his father."

Follow God's example.

This is particularly important when we're thinking of growing in our personal relationships with others. Here especially we need to *pattern our ways of "living in relationship" after God's example.* That is, we need to apply the same principles in our life with our parents, our buddies, our non-Christian acquaintances, and our Christian friends that God applies in living with us.

Some of these ways of living with others are illustrated in Christ's life on earth. Others are illustrated in men like the apostle Paul, who could say, "Be imitators of me, as I am of Christ" (1 Cor. 11:1 RSV). Other ways of living with people are stated in the Bible as principles, as guidelines, for personal relationships.

Like the principle of "love."

Once Jesus laid this out very clearly, showing us that the reason we are to live with others in love is exactly because we are to imitate God. Here's what He said.

> There is a saying, "Love your *friends* and hate your enemies!" But I say, Love your *enemies!* Pray for those who *persecute* you! In that way you will be acting as true sons of your Father in heaven. For He gives His sunlight to both the evil and the good, and sends rain on the just and the unjust too.
>
> If you love only those who love you, what good is that? Even scoundrels do that much! If you are friendly only to your friends, how are you different from anyone else? Even the heathen do that!
>
> But you are to be perfect, even as your Father in heaven is perfect! (Matt. 5:43–48).

So here it is: We are to love others—even our enemies—because this is the way God relates to all men. In love.

We've seen other principles that are, like love, keys to the building of our own personal relationships. For instance, *acceptance.* God accepts us as we are. And we are to first accept ourselves, and then others—as is! Without strings attached. Another we've seen is *forgiveness.* Meaningful and deep relationships are built on extending and receiving forgiving love—not on trying to earn love by doing. (Especially when what others expect us to do to be "in" is wrong!)

Now this kind of living with others, as God does, may look like a pretty tough order. And it may lead to tough times because not everyone will respond to you. After all, not everyone responds to God! But I'm confident that, tough or not, *you can do it.*

Why am I confident that you can?

It's a pretty basic conviction. If you are a Christian and have God's new life in you, He and all His power are present and available to help you become. To enable you to actually apply these principles in your personal relationships, and so to change your relationships with others and to change your very personality! The Bible says, "Loving God means doing what he tells us to do, and really that isn't hard at all; for every child of God can obey him, defeating sin and evil pleasure by trusting Christ to help him" (1 John 5:3–4).

Sure, you'll fail at times. Perhaps a lot of times. But you always have God's forgiving love to fall back on. And you have His new life within to give it a try again.

So now we're down to the basic issue about fitting in. Things like listening, and reflecting, and self-revelation (things we looked at in chap. 2) can help anyone. But what is going to make the real difference—in you, and in the way you fit in with others—is learning to live with them in God's way. It's discovering what God's principles for building relationships are, and then *doing it His way.*

This is what the rest of the chapters in this book are designed to do. They look at various relationships young people are concerned about, and explore principles that apply directly to them. We'll take looks at common problems kids have shared, and see what specific guidelines there are for relating to these special others—like parents, non-Christians, etc.

And then it will all be up to you.

To decide. To decide whether you want to try living with them in God's way, or not.

Whatever you decide as you think the issues through, it's nice to know one thing. As a Christian, you *can do it.*

You can "become."

Steps to take

1. Look over the story of the prodigal (pp. 50-51) again. If his story represents *your* relationship with God, just where do you think you are right now?
   a. at home, but eager to leave
   b. packed up and on the journey away
   c. living it up in the far country with "parties and prostitutes"
   d. miserable, feeding the pigs with the parties all over
   e. coming to your senses and thinking seriously about returning and confessing
   f. determined to come back and confess
   g. welcomed back, knowing you're loved and

accepted and at peace in your relationship with God

2. How might understanding God's forgiving love affect you at the place where you have just indicated you are right now?

3. The author says he is convinced that, as a Christian, you can "become" the kind of person who has warm and helpful relationships with others, the kind of person you want to be.
Why is he so sure you can do it?
How does he think you will have to do it?

5

Parents as people

"To me," writes a college freshman, "one of the major goals in life is to be able to relate with your parents. This was achieved in my family, for my parents were always very honest and open about everything. They devoted their time to listen to me talk when I was happy and when I was depressed. They would offer their opinions on subjects and yet didn't dictate what I should believe. They made me feel wanted and I knew that I could always depend on them. Another thing unique about my parents was that they didn't hide the fact that they were wrong at times and had problems. The things that I learned from their experiences will probably shape the way I conduct my own married and family life."

It's great to have an ideal relationship with parents. Not everyone does. In the best of homes there is at least some conflict.

"Some level of adolescent-parent conflict has been virtually a constant factor in human societies," says an article in a journal on young people.[1] A sampling of the guys and girls who helped me with this book showed that Christian homes are no exceptions. And the kinds of complaints I heard point to one major problem that most seem to have.

"I'm certainly having conflict with parents about clothes," says a high school girl. "Our school dress code was changed so we were able to wear slacks. My parents think that I'm a so-called rebellious teenager because I've worn them twice. I've tried to tell them about it peaceably, but it won't help."

Other girls spoke up on this too. "My guardians feel that our fashions are out of this world," says a sixteen-year-old. "And they don't feel that we know what we're doing. I think if I could learn to fit in better with them that we might have a better relationship. Both sides have a big

stubborn streak, and won't change their ideals or give in the least. But, I think if both of us try to understand the other, we all would be the better for it, and have a close relationship."

That's all right, but a third girl raises another problem: "My parents don't always understand. In my case, they look down on me because they don't like the way I dress, the music I listen to, etc. I guess a lot of times they just don't realize that soon I won't be under their care and I will soon have to live on my own. I think as a teenager you should really prepare for the future and try to be more independent."

Sometimes parents and teens can work toward understanding. "My parents and I have had only one spat," says the daughter of missionaries, "and it wasn't even serious. It was about skirt lengths. Well, we compromised and everything was all right."

But a person doesn't always have parents he or she can talk with. One teen expressed a wish to "Just be able to talk to them without getting mad or backing into an argument."

When communication degenerates into bickering and argument, it's impossible to work toward understanding. "I can't talk to my parents," says a high school guy. "If I were to tell them my ideas and philosophies about certain things, they would be shocked because they are so different from their own. Yet, I have a pretty close relationship with God. But I just can't see being so puritanical about certain things. My parents go to the extreme the other way, so that you really feel out of it."

Now, this sounds like the major problem is over styles and music and things like that. But it's not so. These are just the symptoms that point to the problem.

The process of maturing plants in us an ache to be

trusted and to be given responsibility. This can be expressed in many ways besides the ones we've seen. "They never let me do anything without their permission," is how a sixteen-year-old guy says it. "Like if I want to go out, I have to ask; or if I want to do something or anything, I have to ask, ask, ask." Older teens and those in their twenties feel a need to make up their own minds about some things. And often they feel they have a right to decide some things for themselves (particularly those things which affect their lives with other kids). After all, a person needs some freedom to learn to be responsible.

I'm certainly not against this. But at the same time, I hope we don't demand independence. Because independence isn't really what we need to be mature.

I think you can see why this is so in this story of Ralph's high school days. He set out to fight for independence—and his parents resisted. But, let's let him tell the story himself, and see if it helps us clarify the basic issue:

> I remember when I was in high school and the many problems that I had in this area. I remember my mother saying that the trouble with a lot of parents is that they are afraid of their children. She was more or less determined that she was not going to be one of them. Whereas I solemnly, but unconsciously, set out to show how that even though she wasn't afraid of me, I wasn't afraid of her or my father. By rights I should have been afraid of my father because he could really be violent.
>
> In our home there was a great concern for rules that were to be kept, one of which was that I would be home no later than 12 midnight no matter what the occasion. I objected openly. This was one situation which shows my own increasing desire for independence from my parents.
>
> I was out for sports and therefore there was no problem with the week nights or the night before a game. I felt that in order to do good in sports I should get my rest and consequently I was in bed by 10 each night except

> weekends. This was the big problem.
>
> Each weekend I would go out to the roller skating rink which closed at midnight. I could not stay till they closed and still get home on time. Many times I would deliberately stay out late just to show them that I was old enough to take care of myself.
>
> I can remember week after week my mother wondering how to control me. How could she enforce what she said? She would ask me about it and talk with my brother and sisters about it. I can remember staying out until 2, 3, and even 4 just because I wasn't going to have to follow any silly little rule.
>
> While I was a senior in high school I had pretty well won my victory. My mother openly admitted her defeat. I asked her out of mere formality if it was all right if I went to the junior-senior prom at school. She told me, "I won't tell you that you can go, but I can't stop you either." I went.
>
> She even read up on problems of adolescents. She tried hard to do what was right, and she let us know that she was really concerned for us and loved us. As I think back this was the one thing she did that was "most" right.

Ralph and his mother fought a dogged battle over control. And both lost.

Control?

A recent poll of 660 parents showed that 77 percent feel helpless in trying to carry out the responsibility of guiding their teenagers. And, in many cases, they simply stop trying! Why do some mothers and fathers give up? The report of the survey says,

> Sixty-one percent surrender in the hope that this will make their children love them more; and fifty-six percent said they knuckle under because they fear that if they do not, their children will turn against them.[2]

On the other side are parents like Ralph's, who determine "not to be afraid" of their kids, and who set out to prove it. When a parent offers such a challenge, most teens will do what Ralph did—"solemnly, but unconsciously, set out to show how that even though she wasn't afraid of me, that I wasn't afraid" either. One way or another, relationships between parents and teens seem to become battles over control.

Unfortunately, there really isn't any winner in battles over control. Both sides are going to get hurt, no matter who comes out on top. For conflicts in which one person must dominate the other are destructive of human relationships on both sides. In struggling for dominance, the goal of interdependence is always lost sight of.

Interdependence is a hard thing to understand, and even harder to establish. It's partly because it isn't related to authority, and we tend to try to make it be. You see, interdependence is *not* shared decision-making. Instead, interdependence is the realization that people in relationship always need each other. Each of us needs to give and to receive insights and ideas and feelings and meanings. In open sharing where people come to understand each other, the issues we face together can be better understood. And the decisions that are made (by the person who has that responsibility) can be made in understanding. In love. With concern for the points of view of everyone involved.

Interdependence, then, involves learning to face problems and questions and work them through, together.

This is particularly difficult for parents. All through childhood Mom and Dad have thought of you as a dependent person. They've felt responsible for sitting by your bed when you were sick, for keeping you from eating too much ice cream, for choosing and buying your clothes. Even, on occasion, for whom you played with.

They loved you, and when you were a child they made decisions for you because they knew you had neither the knowledge nor the wisdom to make good decisions for yourself. It's hard for them to realize that now you may know more about some things than they do. That your decisions, if you had the freedom to make them, might be better than theirs.

Ideally, a mom and dad will extend greater and greater responsibility for making decisions as a teen matures. They'll talk things over with him and make sure his reasons for what he wants to do are sound. They'll share their feelings and ideas with him. And, unless convinced that his desires are really out of line, they'll let him go ahead and do it his way, even if it isn't just exactly the way they'd do it themselves.

But not every parent has the self-confidence (or the confidence in his teens) to take this course. And sometimes young people don't make it any easier for parents to relinquish control willingly. "My problem with parents," says an older collegian, "hinged on my need for personal freedom. There were several conflicts over my desire to read intellectually stimulating material, stay out later than 11, express myself in dress, political opinions, etc. In high school they limited my freedom in many ways although they said they trusted me. Now they have pretty much accepted my relative maturity and need for independence, and we have a much better relationship."

There's really nothing you can do to *make* Mom and Dad "accept your relative maturity" and "need for independence." There's nothing you can do to force them toward a better, an interdependent, relationship. But there are several things that can help.

Understanding authority

We all live under authority. Not just teens. Your dad probably works for someone, his boss. As a college professor, I work in an authority framework. The department head, the dean of the graduate school, the faculty senate, and many in the college administration are in positions to make decisions that affect me. Even the self-employed person operates under the limiting authority of government regulations—and these can be very limiting, and very frustrating! So being under authority isn't something that's just for teens and young people in their twenties.

But note what "under authority" means. Simply that other people make decisions that affect and limit me. That the decisions the one in authority makes are decisions that I'm not allowed to make.

The Bible views such an authority system as a good and proper thing. In Romans 13:1 it says, "Obey the government, for God is the one who has put it there." And God put it there to make decisions regarding the lives of people under it, "so those who refuse to obey the laws of the land are refusing to obey God." It goes on to say that "the policeman," the representative of civil authority, "is sent by God to help you. But if you are doing something wrong, of course you should be afraid, for he will have you punished. He is sent by God for that very purpose. So you must obey the laws for two reasons: to keep from being punished and because you know you should."

Somehow human beings, because of that kink inside which God calls sin, are bound to be much worse off without some system of external regulation. Some system that limits the decisions we can make by imposing an authority to make certain decisions for us. And we have to learn to live "under authority."

The authority system hits us from many angles. The

Bible even says, "You slaves must always obey your earthly masters, not only trying to please them when they are watching you but all the time; obey them willingly because of your love for the Lord and because you want to please him. Work hard and cheerfully at all you do, just as though you were working for the Lord and not merely for your masters" (Col. 3:22–23). Written in a day when a great proportion of the population was "owned" by others, the command to obey, even within a clearly unjust system, is striking. And so is God's word to young people: "You children must always obey your fathers and mothers, for that pleases the Lord" (Col. 3:20). "Children, obey your parents for this is right. Honor your father and mother" (Eph. 6:1–2 RSV).

All such injunctions to those *under authority* are accompanied in the Bible by commands to those *in* authority. *Having authority doesn't mean dominating others, or insisting on control of everything they think and feel or do.* To parents, God says, "Don't keep on scolding and nagging your children, making them angry and resentful. But bring them up with the loving discipline the Lord Himself approves, with suggestions and godly advice" (Eph. 6:4). This certainly doesn't sound like the compulsive demand for complete control that authority struggles between parents and teens may become!

But misuse of authority doesn't change the basic issue. For authority can be sinned against from both sides—by those who have it, and those under it! Still, God's way in human society is to rest authority in some roles. The government leader, the employer [a modern-day parallel to the slave owner of biblical times], and the parent, do have the responsibility for making decisions that affect and limit others. And this is right.

When we are under such authority (as a citizen, an

employee, or as a child) we are to obey.

But note a second thing: *Authority is to be exercised and responded to in ways that encourage close personal relationships, ways that permit interdependence.* Neither is to treat the other impersonally, or to act except in love, with full consideration for the other as a person.

It's so easy to violate this vital principle. One teen reports what happens when *persons* are lost sight of in an authority struggle in the home: "Please advise parents," he says, "to be willing to listen. My biggest problem with my folks during high school was that I never was allowed to really vent my side of an argument. As soon as I said something, I was talking back."

When it comes down to a fight over control, something like this is bound to happen. Having to insist on his authority makes the person on top treat the other as less than human. And fighting authority makes the person underneath do the same thing! Personal relationships are destroyed, and both sides lose all potential for growth into interdependence.

The way out

If I were writing to your parents I'd have something different to say here. They're on top, and so I'd suggest right ways of exercising authority that provide a way out of parent-teen conflicts. But I'm writing to you down there on the bottom. So I have to suggest right ways of *responding* to authority—ways that will lead to more and more freedom and responsibility being granted to you.

There is only one framework for right responses: the framework provided by obedience.

Obeying won't solve all your problems at home. It may even create more problems at first. But obedience as a way of living with parents lets you respond to parents as persons, and helps them learn to treat you the same way.

Being successfully obedient requires the application of many interpersonal principles that we've already talked about. Remembering that obeying is the *right* way to respond to parental decisions, we still need to ask, What relationship principles make this a *successful* way to respond?

Forgiving. Parents are only human. And that means they can be wrong. They can even be mean and spiteful—positively sinful. The decisions that affect their children can be made with wrong motives (like trying to "prove" their authority, or to impose their personal preferences in areas that have no moral implications). Their decisions can be poor ones—decisions a young person might make better because he lives in and knows his world better. Even when our parents are not, in fact, wrong, we often feel they are.

Sometimes we feel this deeply. Their decisions hurt us, as they hurt Ruth.

> I love my parents very much and they love me immensely, to the point of being overly protective sometimes. I took Driver Education in high school in my sophomore year. I learned to drive a car and wanted practice. Naturally, I was thrilled; learning to drive was a step toward adulthood. My dad was not the least bit cooperative during this whole period. He just didn't want me to be involved in the danger of traffic and the pressure of driving. When my friends started getting their licenses, I had to beg to get to go out with them. It really hurt me; I assumed my dad's apprehension was based on lack of confidence in me, my driving, and my friends. Of course, this wasn't the case at all, as I look back on it. While I was growing up my dad had to make adjustments too. To him, I was still his little girl that he had always provided transportation for. He found it hard to understand why I would rather drive myself, or ride with a friend who drove.

"It really hurt me." And lots of things during this period are apt to do just this: to hurt you.

How do we react to hurt? Or to what seems to be a "wrong"? One common response pattern is illustrated by the guy who "expressed my feelings by eyeing my parents with hatred." The same pattern in Ralph's case meant "deliberately staying out late just to show them." Both of these are *retaliating* responses. Ways of fighting back. And such ways are strictly ruled out in God's guidelines for living with others.

Talking about Christ, the Bible tells how He "never answered back when insulted; when he suffered he did not threaten to get even; he left his case in the hands of God who always judges fairly" (1 Peter 2:23).

This is an example we are to follow in our personal relationships. "Don't repay evil for evil," the Bible says. "Don't snap back at those who say unkind things about you. Instead, pray for God's help for them, for we are to be kind to others, and God will bless us for it" (1 Peter 3:9). Striking back magnifies our differences. It pits us against each other, causing anger and hurt and, worst of all, leading to bitterness. "Try to stay out of all quarrels," Scripture says, "and seek to live a clean and holy life. . . . Watch out that no bitterness takes root among you, for as it springs up it causes deep trouble, hurting many in their spiritual lives" (Heb. 12:14–15). A retaliating response can only lead to this: bitterness and deep trouble on both sides.

But we have the antidote to bitterness. It's forgiving love. "Now this word to each of you," writes Peter in a book that centers on living under authority, "be as one big family, full of sympathy towards each other; full of love for one another with tender hearts and humble minds" (1 Peter 3:8). Translated into action, that means simply this: "Stop being mean, bad-tempered and angry. Quarreling, harsh words, and dislike of others should have no place in your lives. Instead, be kind to each other, tender-hearted, forgiving one another, just as God has forgiven you because you belong to Christ" (Eph. 4:31–32).

Now just a minute! Does this mean we are to forgive when we're in the right? When Mom and Dad are *wrong?*

It has to.

Because it's *only when we think someone else is doing us wrong that we have the opportunity to forgive them!*

To cleanse our own hearts of bitterness, and to find the freedom from those quarrels and arguments that a grudging obedience is likely to create, we have to learn to forgive.

Listening. "Trying to see things from their viewpoint is so necessary in getting along with parents. It takes a real desire to understand on the part of the parent and teen." What this college student says is a key for relating to parents as persons: "Trying to see things from their viewpoint."

As another twenty-one-year-old says, building really personal relationships with parents is crucial in learning to fit in at home. "Get to know your parents as people: as personalities rather than just thinking of them as authorities."

This isn't always easy to do. "I am definitely not argumentative," says one high schooler, "but when I try to discuss things with my parents, they always argue." This may be true. Or it may be that what she sees as "a discussion" seems to her parents an attempt to outmaneuver them. If things have been on edge at home, almost anything can appear to be an attack. When parents feel under attack, they're likely to retreat from "being persons" to "being authorities," and an argument develops.

So one of the most important ways a teen can help build good relationships at home is by taking the "threat" out of discussions with parents. You know that "Why?" is a pretty fair question. But even "Why?" can sound like (and be!) a challenge to parental authority. Our attitude shows through in our tone of voice, and in the way we look. So "Why?" is best asked when it is motivated by a desire to understand the feelings and ideas of our parents, not as part of our battle over control.

When we ask "Why?" and then settle down to listen (using the ways of listening discussed in chapter 2), we're not likely to get into arguments. And we'll learn a lot about our parents as people.

This is what is important—learning to know others as persons, not as stereotyped roles. At least, I think it is. Because I really buy this interdependence idea. I feel that we *need* to understand the other person's point of view, as well as his feelings and attitudes. This means, on the one hand, that your parents have a lot to offer that you need. Not in terms of orders, but in terms of ways of looking at life. Of insights and values that they've developed through years of living. At this point, *control* isn't the issue at all. The issue is gaining understanding that helps you make your *own* decisions wisely!

So we can add another principle to that of forgiveness for living with parents. It's this: *willingness to understand and learn from others.*

This too is highlighted in Scripture as one of God's ways of living in relationships. "Be humble," the Bible says, "thinking of others as better than yourself. Don't just think about your own affairs, but be interested in others too and in what they are doing" (Phil. 2:3–4).

Humility, that honest desire to understand and learn from others (even to admit that their thinking might at times be better than yours!), creates a nonthreatening atmosphere between people. In this atmosphere we don't have to fight for dominance. In this atmosphere, we're free to communicate as persons.

And, by the way, it's important to remember that the way we respond to the authority of our parents (in obedience rather than with resistance) provides the framework in which we can relate to them this way. Obedience removes the threat and lets us be persons with each other.

Forgiving rather than being bitter, and developing a desire to understand rather than being driven to justify our own opinions—these attitudes create a situation where personal relationships have a chance.

Revealing. This is a third key to building helpful relationships at home: revealing your own feelings and ideas to your folks. This may seem particularly tough just now. Like the parents of one teen I've quoted, your parents may see expressions of your viewpoint as "back talk." Or you may be afraid, as another guy, that "if I were to tell them my ideas and philosophies about certain things, they would be shocked."

But this is just what it takes to build the right kind of relationships at home. Because interdependence works both ways!

Sure, you need your parents' ideas and insights. But they need yours too. Your attitudes, your feelings, your viewpoints, are *needed.* Sharing them is a ministry to your parents.

Obviously, shouting our views at someone isn't ministering to him. No one is going to hear what we say when we shout; he'll sense an attack and resist us.

This is why, again, willingness to obey in any authority

relationship is a necessary prerequisite for communicating. And usually it's a good idea to listen (showing that humility we just read of) before we try to talk. But being willing to lay ourselves out before our parents, to honestly *be ourselves* with them, is the only way we'll find a final solution to tensions at home.

I've already said some things about openness in chapter 2. I'll have more to say later. So for now it may be enough to point out that revealing ourselves is a goal we each have to shoot for and grow toward.

Can do?

This pattern of life with parents, like all the patterns God lays down for personal relationships, is difficult for us. And threatening. It's pretty clear that it means taking risks. The risk of obeying (even when we know a better way). The risk of forgiving (even when we're aware that if we are *too* forgiving, someone might take advantage of us). The risk of listening (even when others might use the opportunity to steamroller us). The risk of sharing honestly (even when our parents might have fears aroused, and then, in fear, limit our freedom even further).

How can we afford to take these risks? By remembering one thing. The same thing the Bible tells us that Christ, our example, counted on in His life on earth. It's in two passages that I've already quoted in this chapter. You don't have to repay evil for evil, the Bible says, because you can "pray for God's help for them, for we are to be kind to others, and God will bless us for it." You don't have to answer back, but can, like Christ, leave your case "in the hands of God." Doing things God's way not only releases His power *in* us. It also frees Him to act *for* us.

Being the kind of person God wants us to be with others, our trust can be placed in God to help *them* become, in response to us, the persons He wants them to be too.

Steps to take

1. A seventeen-year-old from Ohio writes the following. How do you feel about what he says?

   "Do the adults really understand the pressures placed on us teens today? How can they? True, there have been throughout the ages certain universal pressures. Today they seem more intense. So is it really wrong for us to act crazy and do irrational things? Yes, these are rebellious acts, but they only are during youth in most cases. So is it wrong?"

2. The author suggests several concepts which he feels are closely related to parent-teen conflict. How do you feel about each issue when it's related to your own homelife?

   dominance, or control   responsibility
   obedience   authority

3. What do you think now about one key sentence from this chapter: "Authority is to be exercised and responded to in ways that encourage close personal relationships."

4. Look over the lead quote to this chapter (page 59). How like or unlike the situation this person describes is your own homelife?

   Within the framework of obedience, which of the following do you believe would do *most* to make your home *more like* the home described there?

   forgiving?   listening?   revealing?

6 On campus

"How can you talk to people at school," asks a sixteen-year-old girl, "and not only at school but anywhere you are, when you get with people and don't know if they are Christians or if they are just nice persons?"

She seems to reflect an uncertainty that many Christian kids feel. Like the guy (quoted in chapter 1) who said, "During high school I always felt I was separate from the other kids."

We might as well face it. We live in a world where most of our contacts, at school or on the job, will be with others who aren't Christians. And the question of how to relate to them, and how to feel about them, looms pretty big.

It seems to me that the strongest feelings high schoolers and collegians share about relationships at school are *insecurity* and *uncertainty*. Somehow the campus, where you rub shoulders with all sorts of kids, isn't the most comfortable of worlds.

Actually, learning how to fit in on campus puts pressure on everyone, whether they are Christians or not. So it might help some to know that feeling "separate from others" isn't something that you're automatically stuck with when you become a Christian. It really isn't one of those "crosses" we alone have to bear. Still, there are some things that complicate this learning process for Christians. At least, they seem to.

How do other Christian kids talk about the special pressures they feel? Let's give them a chance to speak for themselves.

As a college man recalls it, "Relating to non-Christian kids when they are doing something you don't approve of is hard." He asks, "In a bus coming home from a football game a large group of students are telling dirty jokes or exhibiting improper behavior. How can a Christian signify his disapproval without alienating all of them from himself and his cause?"

Carol, now a student in college, says, "When I study and learn with a certain group of friends all day, I want to get to know all of them well, so that we can feel like a unit and will be able to share things with each other. As a Christian I find myself separated from my non-Christian friends on Friday and Saturday nights (or most social activities) because of my basic convictions on how to please God. When I'm separated from my friends on social occasions, I really don't get to know them as a full person, and vice versa. Many times there are no Christian activities to take the place of activities of my non-Christian friends, and they feel sorry for me because I seem to be living such a dull life. I need social activities in which I can freely participate and also be with my friends—then they can get to know my whole personality and see how Christ *can* (in a positive way) affect my life."

The need for varied social contacts was also seen by Ken, who both raises questions and suggests answers:

"Because I don't condone the actions and ideas of others, does this mean I can't or shouldn't associate with them? On the more practical level, because I don't drink does it mean I don't go to a party where alcohol is served? Or because I don't condone bad language, does this mean I can't associate with those who do?"

Ken doesn't think so. And he finds high school sports a great leveler. "This is the advantage of athletics and even the system of academics and grades—a Christian is a co-equal. He can be himself, he need not be critical of others, and he feels more at home.

A Christian can't even begin to be a Christian influence unless he can associate with non-Christians—even become their friends and a part of their activities. And yet this makes being a good example really difficult."

Several kids spoke of extra-curricular activities as partially able to bridge this difficulty. "I was quite active in high school, and one of my activities was chorus," shares Alayne. "Next to me on each side were two girls who eventually became close friends, and because we fit in and had lots of fun, they eventually wanted to know what I really believed and why. Of course, they wanted to go to Campus Life too, but one gal ran into trouble at home because she was Jewish. But both were interested and one believed. Most important, I found I was trying to see the other person's viewpoints and trying not only to accept them, but to understand them."

Alayne and Ken do give at least partial solutions. You don't have to get totally involved in a non-Christian's pattern of life to become friends. But you do need to take advantage of all the neutral situations you can—things like sports and chorus and socials that don't violate your convictions—to get to know others and let them know you. Still, it's not easy. As Helen, another high schooler, says of her attempts at friendship, "I try to stay on their subject and try to be their friend, even though they are talking about something that I myself don't care to talk about. But how would I try to talk about God? I mean, if there was a guy in my class, and I wanted to make friends with him, so that maybe I could share my testimony about God, and all he talked about was smoking grass, how would I go about trying to tell him the Word of God?"

This is another thing that seems to make special problems for the Christian. Many want to "fit in" for a purpose. "Being able to fit in well with a non-Christian is essential for a Christian," says Cathy, a sixteen-year-old from North Dakota. "If a Christian wishes to witness, I think that it is necessary to get along with the person. It would be awfully hard to tell a person about God and to try to give your testimony if you couldn't get along with the person."

The feeling that friendships outside the faith are a means to an end (witnessing) puts on added pressure. We aren't only worrying how to fit in; we're concerned about how to get in a word for the Lord.

Put together all these pressures—the fact that convictions often cut you off from the social activities of your schoolmates, that the things some do and say make you wonder if you should associate with them at all, and the worry about how to share Christ with them once you do get to know them—and they make the normal task of learning to relate to others far more difficult.

Being friends

In a way, it's not finding answers to the "technical" problems in building such relationships that makes the real trouble for us. I mean, there are ways of making time and opportunity for building friendships with non-Christians. After all, "being friends" doesn't mean that people spend *all* their time together! All it means is that we like and enjoy each other, and to some extent come to know each other as persons. And this can happen in lots of situations. In class, in school clubs, in sports, on the school newspaper, and so on. We can start friendships while standing in the halls by our lockers, and when we go to the games to cheer for the school team. We can take part in socials that *don't* violate our convictions—and even plan our own.

Sure, having Christian convictions places limits on some of the things you'll want to do with others, *but it's really not these limitations that cut you off from non-Christians!* For every guy you know who squats in the hall to smoke grass and cuss, there are three or four (or more) who quietly go about their business. For every "in" gal whose life is tied up in a round of social activities your convictions cut you out of, there are three or four (or more) who are actually lonely—who don't have much social life at all. If we want to be honest, we have to admit that on every campus there are plenty of kids who want, and need, friends. Whatever else it may be, campus society isn't one big conspiracy of non-Christians with plenty of friends taking great delight in discovering who the Christians are so they can cut them off.

If it's not the limitations our convictions impose that keep us from being friends with non-Christian kids, what is it? Mostly it is the *feelings* and *attitudes about others* that develop when our convictions and beliefs make us feel "different" from them. What cuts us off is far more likely to be *inside us* than outside us in the real social limitations our faith imposes.

Now, it's perfectly normal to react to things some kids say and do that we know are wrong. It's perfectly normal to pull back. It's perfectly normal to be uncertain, even repelled. But then we have to fight through our *reactions* to develop basic attitudes toward these kids and others. Tragically, we Christians often develop attitudes which cut us off—from all the kids at school, and not just the ones we reacted to at first. You can see common attitudes reflected in these quotes from the fellows and girls who helped me write this book. Remember, these are actual quotes. Just look at a few and see if you can pick up some of the basic attitudes toward others that have developed.

"Non-Christians don't accept me because I'm too mature and feel differently as far as religion goes. At school I don't try to get into cliques because it's not worth it."

"I don't know. I don't seem to care very much about fitting in. I really don't. But love is a bond, and I suppose if you ask God to do it, I think you'll come out OK."

"The non-Christians around me seem so foolish and lost. I, as a Christian, often find myself becoming too high-minded because I was "smart" enough to know God when I saw Him. I realize that this is a completely wrong attitude toward non-Christians, but still I often find myself in this sort of arrogance."

"I want to be frank. In high school I stuck to my church group. I didn't want to be with non-Christians. I wanted nothing to do with them. Why? Because my interests were on church affairs and not their parties and doings. Thus, I never took the time to really get to know a non-Christian, so I never found any mutual interests. You see, in this way I excluded possibilities to witness to them about Christ."

"My problem is one of learning to get along with kids at school. Perhaps one of inferiority. Other teenagers perhaps do not understand what I feel because for them moving means from one state to another, or city to city. I moved here from another country. I find it hard to relate in school."

"I'm not accepted at school because of my looks; my grades (A's); my actions (I'm considered a goody-goody). For example, I am roll-taker in chorus and must give out tardy slips. A couple days ago, a girl asked me for one so she could be late to biology and then just present the slip and get off the hook. I said NO and immediately lost a friend."

What do these quotes say to you?

They say a lot to me.

No, not that the kids who say these things are real stinkers, and ought to be ashamed. Not that. What they tell me is that we respond to the special campus pressures on a

Christian by building walls instead of bridges. That, under pressure, we can develop attitudes toward non-Christians that become an unconscious excuse for failures to build friendships.

Insurmountable barriers do go up when our first feelings of differentness become, in time, feelings of superiority ("I'm too mature," and all the campus crowd is "so foolish and lost") or of special holiness (because you don't "want to be with non-Christians" and dedicate yourself to "church affairs and not their parties and doings"). It's just as harmful when our first feelings grow into a sense of inferiority ("I'm so inferior and misunderstood") or unconcern ("I just don't care to make friends with them"). When our feelings of uncertainty harden into basic attitudes like these, we find it impossible to break through in our contacts with others. Why? *Because our attitudes show through.* When deep inside we reject the people we talk to, that rejection is felt by them—no matter what we say.

Remember Miss Goody-goody? Who said no to a request for a tardy slip? She was certainly right to say no. But if she "lost a friend" the reason wasn't what she said, but the way she said it. If her "no" implied condemnation for making a wrong request, the other girl felt it. When you feel and talk "down" to a person, you'll never become friends.

Sorting it out

I suppose most of us feel that the attitudes just illustrated and described aren't quite right. But we still don't know just how a Christian *should* feel about non-Christians.

To sort this out, let's go back to our key principle for learning how to relate. Remember it? "Follow God's example in everything you do." If we follow His example, how will we feel about others, and how will we relate to them? We can know because God came into our world and lived among sinners—just as we're called to do. We can know because we can discover how Christ acted when He was on earth. And the first thing we want to ask is this: Did Jesus cut Himself off from sinners?

Cut Himself off? Hardly! In fact, the "religious" people of His day complained that He hung around with the worst sort of sinners (Matt. 11:19)! Take this incident:

> As he [Jesus] was walking up the beach he saw Levi, the son of Alphaeus, sitting at his tax collection booth. "Come with me," Jesus told him. "Come be my disciple!" And Levi jumped to his feet and went along! That night Levi invited many of his fellow tax gatherers and other notorious sinners as his dinner guests to meet Jesus and his disciples. (There were many men of this type among the crowds that followed him.)
>
> But when some of the Jewish religious leaders saw him eating with these men of ill repute, they said to his disciples, "How can he stand it, to eat with such scum?" When Jesus heard what they were saying, he told them, "Sick people need the doctor, not healthy ones! I haven't come to tell good people to repent, but the bad ones" (Mark 2:14–17).

Interesting, isn't it? Here was Jesus taking the initiative to build relationships with "notorious sinners." And here were many "men of this type" actually drawn to Him. Actually seeking His company!

Surprising? That sinners would be drawn to a really good man? Another story may illustrate why. One day the religious leaders brought Jesus a woman caught in adultery, to see what He would do. The Bible tells us that they insisted, since she had sinned, that He say whether she should be stoned to death (which by the law would have been right) or not.

> But Jesus stooped down and wrote in the dust with his finger. They kept demanding an answer, so he stood up again and said, "All right, hurl the stones at her until she dies. But only he who never sinned may throw the first!" Then he stooped down again and wrote some more in the dust.
>
> And the Jewish leaders slipped away one by one, beginning with the eldest, until only Jesus was left in front of the crowd with the woman. Then Jesus stood up again and said to her, "Where are your accusers? Didn't even one of them condemn you?"
>
> "No, Sir," she said.
>
> And Jesus said, "Neither do I. Go and sin no more" (John 8:6–11).

Certainly Jesus (unlike you and me, who have our share of sins) had the *right* to condemn. He had the right to throw the first stone, the right to criticize. But He didn't. He acted toward her *in forgiving love.*

It's important to get this straight. Forgiving love doesn't condone sin, or share in it. (Jesus didn't do that. He said, "Go and sin no more.") But forgiving love *does* accept and express care for the person who sins! And whatever else the "many men of this type" thought about Christ, they were drawn to Him because they *felt* His loving concern.

It's easy for us to go wrong at just this point and to tie our feelings about the person to our feelings about his actions. To get the idea that "separation" means keeping away from sinful people as well as sinful actions. Paul had to clear this up with some in his day who became mixed up on this and started to condemn and withdraw from unsaved people. He writes,

> When I wrote to you before I said not to mix with evil people. But when I said that I wasn't talking about unbe-

> lievers who live in sexual sin, or are greedy cheats and thieves and idol worshipers. For you can't live in this world without being with people like that. What I meant was not to keep company with anyone who claims to be a brother Christian but indulges in sexual sins, or is greedy, or is a swindler, or worships idols, or is a drunkard, or abusive. Don't even eat lunch with such a person. It isn't our job to judge outsiders. But it certainly is our job to judge and deal strongly with those who are members of the church, and who are sinning in these ways (1 Cor. 5:9–12).

See what the Bible is saying? Not drop out of the campus society because it's populated with non-Christians. The whole world is! No, in fact, the Christian is to mix, even with "evil people." Why? Because *it's not our job to judge these outsiders. It's our job to come to them, as Christ came to us, with forgiving love.*

Being truly good isn't criticizing others. It's caring for them!

Solutions?

No, not yet.

But we have a basis for working out solutions. In discovering the basic attitude toward unbelievers that fits our faith, we can find freedom from the feelings and responses that cut us off from friendships with them. What kinds of freedom do we find in the example of Christ?

Freedom from the need to criticize. We often feel a compulsion to criticize (or at least feel critical of) others who do wrong things. A feeling that we ought to "do something" when someone tells a dirty joke to let them know we think they're awful. Usually what comes out is criticism and that's something about which Jesus tells us, "Don't."

That's right. "Don't criticize," He said, "and then you won't be criticized! For others will treat you just as you treat them" (Matt. 7:1–2).

This warning against criticism doesn't mean that we have no right to take a stand. We ought to. But when we do, it helps us to remember that the Bible says, "It's not our job [business] to *judge* outsiders" (1 Cor. 5:12). So we are to take our stand *and* avoid judging or criticizing those who do what we are rejecting.

This isn't exactly easy. But it can be done. Three days ago I dropped into a little grocery where we often shop, located just a block from our high school. There, prominently displayed on the counter, was a well-known sex magazine, its cover splashed with nudes. It really disturbed me to see it in our neighborhood store, so as I chatted with the new owner and his wife I tried to tell them how I felt. The man was defensive at first. After all, he was in business to make money, and the magazines did sell. But when they saw I wasn't attacking or condemning them, both became more open. The wife told how she kept it off the magazine rack, and did care who they sold copies to. I shared how, working nights in a motel, I had closed down the magazine stand rather than sell this kind of book, and why I'd felt as I did. We talked about other things too: what they'd done before they took over the store, the country they had come from a dozen years before. But most important to me, I found the Lord taking judgment of them out of my own heart, and replacing it with interest in them as persons.

I dropped into the store yesterday. The magazines were still there. But as soon as I turned down an aisle, the wife turned them over so the front covers did not show.

And I thought this was good. My sharing had made them think.

In telling us that we are not to judge, God is also reminding us that it isn't our place to *force* another person to live by our convictions. Each person is responsible for himself and for his own actions. At best I can only love others and share my feelings honestly—not to criticize or put them down, but to show that I accept and respect them enough to be honest with them about myself.

When I understand that I have not been appointed another's judge (for God alone is to judge outsiders), I'm free to be myself with them without criticism, and in love.

Perhaps Karen explains it best: "During my senior year in high school, I made some non-Christian friends who I could find myself relating to. I found my love growing as I learned to accept them for what they were—not for what I thought they should be. Just be concerned about people; listen to them, but don't force your ideas on them. Be objective about people and don't make prejudgments, but get to know a person first of all." That's what Karen learned. And it's important for all of us.

Freedom from fear of caring. Knowing that we're not responsible to judge others helps us find freedom to know them as persons. We realize that we can be with unbelievers, and *like* them, without feeling guilty about it. We can care for them because, first of all, they are persons.

It's important to learn to think of others as persons—not to stereotype them as "different" or as "sinners." God's way really is to focus on the worthwhileness of each individual (a worthwhileness we thought about back in chapters 3 and 4). And *we* can do this too—without being afraid. This is what Jayne refers to in giving this advice on relating to unbelievers: "Try to develop a love for people just because each person is a unique individual in himself. We must learn not to judge a person from a first impression. After all, we may really look odd to others too. It is intriguing to look at a person and say This individual has a hidden treasure within him; he is wonderful. It's amazing how the whole world seems to change."

So we really can be free. Free to live by our convictions, and to live with others who do not share them. Free both to live *right* and to live *love.* To "lovingly follow the truth at all times—speaking truly, dealing truly, living truly—and so become more and more in every way like Christ" (Eph. 4:15).

Steps to take

1. The author suggests that the basic issue in relating to non-Christians is our attitude toward them. How would you express "the basic attitude toward unbelievers that fits our faith" (p. 98)?

2. How do you explain the eagerness of sinful people to associate with Jesus (p. 96)? What's the situation in your school—are the others eager to associate with you and other Christians? Why, or why not?

3. The author suggests that the "technical" problems of building non-Christian friendships (things like finding time and opportunity for social contact) can be solved if we want to solve them. Jot down all the ways and all the opportunities you can think of to get to know schoolmates and neighbors.

4. What do you think the author should do if the store continues to sell the magazine and display it as before (p. 99)? How can we continue to love people and yet take a firm stand on our convictions? What would *you* do?

7

Speaking out

Getting our attitude toward unbelieving acquaintances in line with Christ's attitude will help us relate to them as persons. But this isn't a total solution to the problems raised by the kids in the last chapter. In our relations with non-Christians we're concerned about more than being friends. We're concerned about communicating Christ.

Here's what a sixteen-year-old says about that: "It's so hard for me to communicate to non-Christian kids because of what they might say about me. We can show them by our actions, but sometimes they might think that a Christian wouldn't do that. Sometimes you just don't know how to put things. Like telling someone about Christ in school. Kids like you OK, but they think you're dumb for saying things like that."

It's not always easy to find the kind of freedom we thought about in the last chapter—freedom to like and to build relationships with non-Christians without compromising our own convictions.

But most of my correspondents saw this as an essential

first step in speaking out for Christ. Remember what Cathy from North Dakota had to say on this? "Being able to fit in well with a non-Christian, is essential for a Christian. If a Christian is to witness, I think that it is necessary to get along with the person. It would be awfully hard to tell a person about God and to try to give your testimony if you couldn't get along with the person."

A collegian makes it even stronger: "Only through a *close friendship* could one of my friends see that God was real."

He's right. They won't listen (would you?) to a guy who stands *outside* their lives and throws stones at them. That fearing, rejecting, judging attitude we saw in the last chapter has got to go. And in its place we need to let God put acceptance of and interest in our campus acquaintances as persons. We ourselves need to take first steps toward friendship by showing ourselves to be friendly. And for this, all those skills we talked about in chapter 2 have a significant place.

So being friends—or at least friendly—really is the first step toward speaking out.

Step two?

There's something else that is important for sharing Christ with campus friends. That is being the right kind of person, the kind who is "truly good."

Teens and youth in their twenties say this in a variety of ways. "Not 'preaching' to non-Christians," one guy says, "but letting Christ—through you—show them you're not a lot of hot air." Another calls it "sharing Christ in a soft-sell sort of way; letting them see Him in me, and thus wanting Him, without me forcing my way of life on them." The Bible talks a lot about this aspect of witnessing—not as a substitute for speaking out, but as

a kind of backdrop for it.

Peter warns us: "Be careful how you behave among your unsaved neighbors; for then, even if they are suspicious of you and talk against you [as many kids feel unbelievers do!], they will end up praising God for your good works when Christ returns" (1 Peter 2:12). And Paul writes in Thessalonians, "This should be your ambition: to live a quiet life, minding your own business and doing your own work, just as we told you before. As a result people who are not Christians will trust and respect you" (1 Thess. 4:11–12).

Actually, trust and respect are the very best bases for acceptance by others. A lot better than trying to gain acceptance by conforming. It really gains you a lot more than going along with the crowd when personal convictions would be violated.[2] You can be "truly good" *and* well liked!

So it is going to be a great help to your witness if you can say with the apostle, "We have proved ourselves to be what we claim by our wholesome lives and by our understanding of the Gospel and by our patience. We have been kind and loving and filled with the Holy Spirit" (2 Cor. 6:6).

But what if we can't say this? What if there are "holes" in our lives, failures where the kinks in our personalities have shown through?

When this happens, do we have to shut up? Even worse, are we supposed to pretend? To put on a front with the kids so we look like we're perfect?

The question of whether a Christian is to try and keep his problems and failings hidden from others is a tough one. To answer it we need to remember one thing.

A Christian is "becoming." We are *in the process of* being transformed by God into Christ's likeness. We're on the way. When we accept and keep on accepting Christ's forgiving love, releasing our cleansed selves to God's power within us, we see real changes in our lives—and so do others.

But becoming implies incompleteness. We haven't arrived. We're not like Christ yet. So we are going to fail at times. We're not *always* going to be "victorious." While we can accept ourselves at times like these (and know Christ accepts us), should we be willing to reveal our problems and failings to others? Especially to non-Christians, to whom we're supposed to be an example? It's at this point that I agree completely with a collegian who advises, "Be a real person—honest and sincere *in all things*." We have to be honest with others about ourselves, even when it shows that we aren't perfect. And even when it shows we're vulnerable.

There are two important reasons why this is true:

1. *The only way we can become close to others, as we saw in chapter 2, is to reveal ourselves to them.* And the selves we reveal have to be the real us. Phoniness cuts us off from each other and destroys relationships. If friendship with unbelievers is important in witnessing, and it is, we just have to be *real* with them—even when this shows that we're vulnerable to the same problems and weaknesses as they are.

2. *The only way we can represent Christianity accurately to unbelievers is to reveal ourselves to them.* When a person accepts Christ all his problems aren't automatically solved, and his sinful nature doesn't just dissolve away. Our whole lives will be lived with that kink of sin inside, and it will break out at the most inopportune times! But relationship with God isn't based on our sinlessness. It's based on His loving forgiveness, given to us in Jesus Christ.

Since witnessing is presenting Christ and a relationship with Christ to others, we need to lay it out the way it actually is. We need to show that God's love, *not* our goodness, is the heart of the gospel. So we need to keep a couple of things in balance: the actual fact that God *is* transforming us (something others will see in our lives), and the secret of our relationship with Him—His forgiving love. We don't want to fail and to be less than loving and righteous. But when we do we can afford to be honest and show others our vulnerablility and our weaknesses. And to ask forgiveness of those our actions might have hurt, because in this way they'll see the reality of God's forgiveness at work in us.

I'll never forget one of my grad students, a pastor's daughter from Indiana, who told me that all through high school she thought of her unbelieving acquaintances as being very "different" from her. Then in her senior year she worked on the school newspaper, and was amazed to discover that the kids who worked with her were so much *like* her, with so many of the same feelings and problems and needs. Maybe it works the other way around. Maybe the non-Christians think of *us* as "different." Maybe, in discovering we're so much like them, with so many of the same feelings and problems and needs, they'll also discover that Christ *can* make a difference after all.

When you live honestly with others, showing love *and* your own vulnerability, you're truly free to do just what the Bible says about speaking out. Then you can "quietly trust yourself to Christ your Lord and if anybody asks why you believe as you do, be ready to tell him and do it in a gentle and respectful way. Do what is right; then, if men speak against you calling you evil names, they will become ashamed of themselves for falsely accusing you when you have only done what is good" (1 Peter 3:15–16).

The gentle way

Reading the Bible I get the impression that speaking out for Christ wasn't any easier when it was written than it is today. Even the apostle Paul had to ask for prayer: "Pray that I will be bold enough to tell it freely and fully, and make it plain, as of course I should," he asked friends at Colosse when he encouraged them to "make the most of your chances to tell others the Good News" (Col. 4:4–5).

What are some of the things that make witnessing seem hard to guys and girls today? Here are some things my friends have mentioned:

The unwillingness of others to talk about religious things. "My girl friend was telling me about the movie she went to Saturday, and the dance on Sunday," says a seventeen-year-old. "Then she asked me what I did on Sunday, and I told her about church. And as soon as I started talking about Young People's, she went on telling me of the movie again, like I'm going to tell her all these different things that we do and then bug her until she comes to the Young People's group."

The tendency to fall into argument. A high school guy says, "In school sometimes we run into non-Christians and it is hard to talk with them because they won't accept your faith and constantly argue with you against it."

A girl adds, "In my opinion, Christian kids have the most trouble relating to non-Christians because non-Christian kids always have something to knock down. They don't give us a chance to say what we want to, or they try to baffle us with turned-around phrases and misquotes from the Bible."

The unwillingness of others to change. A high schooler says, "I have heard one person witness to a Jew and I tried to witness to a person who felt science was the answer in life. In both cases it was hard for them to realize that Christ was the Truth; or, if they did recognize it, they didn't want to admit it." Anytime a person feels that to agree with you he has to admit he's wrong, it's really tough for him!

The difficulties we have in expressing ourselves. "I always have a problem with relating my Christian convictions to my non-Christian friends. To me the Christian life is so exciting and something I want to share with my friends, yet whenever the opportunity comes up, I get all tongue-tied and scared." Kids who felt that a Christian needed to study up on the philosophies of others were reflecting that same insecurity. We might not say what we want to well enough; we might even get pinned by questions we can't answer.

Is there a way out of problems like these? A couple of Scripture passages give us some very helpful guidelines. Some hints on how to witness—the gentle way.

Here's a passage that describes the gentle way to witness. See what you think it means for us.

> Again I say, don't get involved in foolish arguments which only upset people and make them angry. God's people must not be quarrelsome; they must be gentle, patient teachers of those who are wrong. Be humble when you are trying to teach those who are mixed up concerning the truth. For if you talk meekly and courteously to them they are more likely, with God's help, to turn away from their wrong ideas and to believe what is true. Then they will come to their senses and escape from Satan's trap of slavery to sin which he uses to catch them whenever he likes, and they can begin doing the will of God (2 Tim. 2:23–26).

Several things stand out for me. One is the attitude we are to hold toward others when we speak out for Christ. It's shown in words like gentleness, patience, humility, meekness, and courtesy. There's no feeling of argument here, no feeling that when we speak out we're in a fight in which someone must win (by converting the other guy) and the other must lose (by admitting he was wrong).

Another thing that hits me is the lack of pressure on the believer. Sure he speaks out, but he doesn't push the other person. "Coming to their senses" depends on God's help, not the believer's brilliance.

There is one other passage that helps us. It says that the "riches and glory" of God's plan, and the center of our sharing, is this: "that Christ in your hearts is your only hope of glory." So the apostle Paul says of his witnessing, "Everywhere we go and to all who will listen we preach Christ; warning them and teaching them as well as we know how. We want to be able to present each one to

God, perfect because of what Christ has done for each of them" (Col. 1:27–28). This tells us what we have to talk *about*.

Remembering that what we just read presupposes friendly and good relationships with those we speak to, we can find some really helpful guidelines here.

Let's focus on Christ. While it's important to be able to explain different aspects of our belief (one very good reason we need to study the Bible), it's still true that the heart of what we have to say is about Jesus Christ. It's His forgiving love that frees us from our fears, inadequacies and sins, and that opens us up to God's power for change.

So when someone wonders what we believe, and why we act as we do, let's tie our answers directly to Him.

Let's share, not demand. Sometimes we come on too strong in our attempts to witness. We may feel the pressure of responsibility, or just eagerness to let our friends in on a good thing. But when our witnessing seems to *demand* a response from the other person, we're way off the mark. Talking meekly and courteously, and sharing what Christ means to us, really is "more likely" (as the Bible says) to help him turn away from wrong ideas and experience Christ's forgiving love.

You've probably felt the reason why this is true. Has someone ever tried to push you into a decision? Usually when this happens we tighten up inside and start thinking of all the reasons why we don't want to do what he seems to be trying to make us do. The more the pressure is put on, the greater the resistance. It's here that arguments usually start—not with disagreement, but with the feeling that "I've got to resist!"

Ideally, the opportunity to witness comes not when we're talking about our ideas, but when we're sharing ourselves—friend to friend—in a give-and-take relationship. This is implied in a verse we saw earlier: "Quietly trust yourself to Christ your Lord and if anybody asks you why you believe as you do, be ready to tell him and do it in a gentle and respectful way." The other guy started it! This doesn't mean that we're not to take other opportunities to witness. It simply means that living our lives with others is exactly what *gives us* the best opportunities! When others know us as real persons and as friends they're going to begin to wonder, and care, about why we believe as we do.

So sharing, without pressuring the other person, is the gentle (and the best!) way to witness.

Let's relax, and trust God. While you and I have the job of sharing Christ with others, we do *not* have the job of converting them. God does that Himself. As one passage says, the whole package of salvation, from God's forgiving love to our faith in accepting it, is not sourced in ourselves; "It is the gift of God" (Eph. 2:8 AV). So that little phrase "with God's help" in our "gentle witness" passage really is a key one. Knowing this, we needn't feel guilty if someone doesn't respond right away when we share Christ. And we don't need to push another person. We can trust God to help him believe, in His own time and in His own way.

Knowing how to relate to unbelievers in sharing Christ doesn't solve all the problems, of course. We still may have doubts about how to best express ourselves, or how to answer questions they're most likely to ask. (For help on things like this I recommend a good book called *How to Give away Your Faith* by Paul Little.*)

What building friendships will do is help us get close enough to others so what we have to say will be heard.

*Paul Little, *How to Give away Your Faith* (Wheaton, Ill.: Scripture Press, 1966).

And it will free us to share, simply and gently, the reality of our relationship with Christ.

Steps to take

1. If "God's help" is so vital in helping a person respond to our witness to Christ, what can you do besides sharing to help?
2. Read over each of the problems mentioned about witnessing recorded on pages 96–97. How might the "gentle way" guidelines suggested on pages 98–101 help in each case?
3. Here are some quotes from kids, not yet used in this book. Underline what seem to you key phrases or thoughts in what each says, and jot down *why* you agree or disagree with each.

   "As a Christian, I feel probably the most important thing for me to remember is that just because I am a Christian, I am no more or no better than my unsaved friend. Secondly, it's important to open yourself up and be honest with the impression you give the other person because it's almost impossible to keep on filling a role if it's not really yourself."

   "Be considerate of others—think how they feel about something. If you don't agree, don't put on a *front* and pretend you do; rather, express your reasons for your opinions without pressuring the others into it."

   "Because I wasn't verbally witnessing much at school, was I witnessing at all? I found my life spoke very loudly during my high school years so that in my senior year my friend and I brought many kids to the Lord because we had a background which was clean and admirable. Our words were backed up by our past actions. Actions are so important, yet are not emphasized enough."

8

Get a little

Sometimes the whole thing seems overwhelming. Like a person is expected to give a lot more than he's got! Anyway, that's the impression I get from what this college girl advises: "Have an enthusiastic and daily commitment to Christ as your basis for action," she begins, and goes on: "Be involved in activities through which to learn more about Jesus, and then put the love of Christ into practice by accepting, listening to, and offering friendship to kids at school and other individuals. Also, I feel a Christian kid should be well-informed about politics, drugs, music, clothes styles, and be able to understand ideas commonly held by non-Christians even when he doesn't agree. A Christian kid should also challenge his faith and make sure he has a real basis for his beliefs and facts to back them up."

Not that there's anything wrong with this advice. In fact, it's real good. But if a person is supposed to *give* so much in personal relationships, there ought to be some way to *get*, too.

"I learned the importance of developing close Christian friendships this summer when I had my first *really* close friend and saw how we could talk about anything and everything; and because of our Christian love for each other, all barriers were broken down and we really communicated completely." What was the result of this kind of relationship? "My spiritual life was strengthened because of this relationship."

This high school girl brings out the other side of personal relationships. While coming closer to others is the best way we can *give* to them, it's also the best way we can *receive.* Close friendships are something we each *need.*

Lots of fellows and girls told how deeper friendships met needs. "Sometimes," writes a college girl, "I feel a need to communicate my really close feelings to someone besides myself. I need to tell others what I think and hope in order to know myself better."

Other benefits of closeness were mentioned. From a college man: "If you can develop one or two close relationships with others and a strong relationship with God, all the rest slips into place. A strong bond of confidence here allows you to examine your true feelings and desires with others, that will contribute to healthy relations with others."

And from a high schooler: "In order to fit in, it seems necessary to have a close relationship to God and other Christians. Not only Christian teens but older people so when you're not with teens you just don't stand around like a dud. It is necessary to make friends with Christian teens because it makes Christian boy-girl relationships come easier, and also helps you get much closer to God by watching other teens and comparing their lives to yours."

A person can have a lot of friends, but that close, intimate relationship these fellows and girls are talking about is something else. Something beyond. Carl, a high schooler who stood for his faith *and* built friendships with his non-Christian classmates, knows it isn't easy to be constantly giving out without having any recharging relationships. "For several years," he writes, "I did not have any friend of the same sex in whom to confide, and believe me, it is nerve-racking to try to stand up for what you believe when there is no one else who has the same convictions as you. I think this a problem with teenagers today, that we don't have real close friendships of the same sex, to talk over problems. Thanks to Jesus Christ, I was able to build some my senior year."

Something beyond

This recharging kind of friendship is something every Christian needs—and something that is planned and provided for us. It's taken care of, potentially, when a person comes to know Christ as Savior. It's taken care of by coming at that time into a unique relationship with other Christians. Even if relationships with other Christians haven't meant much to you yet, that unique closeness is really there, and experiencing it is open to you.

The Bible talks a lot about our relationship to other Christians and what this can mean to us. "We who believe," it says in Ephesians 2:21, "are carefully joined together. . . as parts of a beautiful, constantly growing temple for God . . . joined in with him and with each other by the Spirit." As "members of God's very own family, citizens of God's country, you belong in God's household with every other Christian" (Eph. 2:19).

You *belong* with other Christians.

This is important to remember. Building friendships with non-Christians, being interested in them, and caring for them and sharing with them, is important. But we must look for the "beyond" kind of relationship—the one that recharges us—with other believers only. One reason for this is that we actually do belong with them. We have so much in common. We're part of the same family, God's family, and that makes us brothers and sisters. Having all this in common, our shared love for God can help us love and trust each other uniquely. As one girl quoted earlier said, "Because of our Christian love for each other, all barriers were broken down and we really communicated completely," with the result that "my spiritual life was strengthened."

Here's the second big reason why our closest relationships need to be with other Christians: None of us is expected to make it as a believer alone. God knows that living the Christian life, sharing our faith with non-Christians, and working out our problems is far beyond our own ability. So He's provided help. He's planned for a truly interdependent relationship between believers!

Earlier we saw that *interdependence* involves giving and taking. Helping and being helped. Supporting and encouraging others when they need it, and being supported and encouraged when we need it. This is exactly the kind of help our belonging with other Christians can mean for us. According to the Bible, our family relationships with other Christians, and our place in the family, have been carefully designed to let us help and be helped. It works out much like a body works. Each part of our body has something important to contribute to the health of the whole. Well, each of us as a Christian has something important to contribute to other believers' lives. And we've been given just the personalities and special abilities we need to do our helping jobs! The apostle Paul sums up one discussion of this "body" idea this way: "Now here is what I am trying to say: All of you together are the one body of Christ and each one of you is a separate and necessary part of it" (1 Cor. 12:27).

That we are each necessary can be a pretty encouraging thought. You or I may get discouraged about our lack of talent or ability as compared with someone else. We may not be as smart, or as clear a talker. Or even as friendly, concerned, or compassionate. Still, we are important and needed. "We are all parts of it [Christ's body]," Romans says, "and it takes every one of us to make it complete, for we each have different work to do. So we belong to each other, and each needs all the others'' (Rom. 12:4–5). There is, then, a very special kind of relationship open to us with other Christians, and experiencing this relationship is the key to our growing and maturing in our faith (cf. Eph. 4:16). If we're going to be able to give a little to others, we need to get a lot from our fellow believers.

It's at this point that I have to bring up the church because *church* is another name for *body* in the Bible. Unfortunately, *church* isn't too popular with some young people today, and that makes church hard to talk about. On the one hand, I don't want that word *church* to bring to your mind the meetings and organizations and activities you call ''going to church.'' Because the biblical focus of ''church'' is on *Christian people and their relationships with each other,* not on the institution or on meetings. On the other hand, I don't want to give you the impression that the church you go to isn't ''the church.'' It is. The adults, the guys and girls in your youth group, the elders and pastor and *everyone* are parts of that ''one body'' with you. So when I talk about belonging and being needed, I really do mean belonging *there* and being needed *by them*—all of them. And I mean needing them too. Somehow that church you go to and the kids you know there are to be the center of recharging relationships for you, a source of love and closeness that can support you and give you what you need so you can give to others.

Now, all this may sound rather ideal. From the things fellows and girls share with me I get the impression that many kids don't find this kind of warmth and acceptance and interdependence with other Christians. But that doesn't make this biblical idea of the church as ''people in helping relationship'' unrealistic. I mean, some parents fight a lot, or show favoritism, or don't seem willing to listen to their children, or any number of other things like this. If you happen to have a home like this, does that mean you're ready to give up on marriage as unrealistic? That you say, "Not for me, man! It sounds ideal, but it's all a fake"? Of course not! Instead, what you say is, "I'm not going to let *my* marriage get like that. I'm going to work at making my marriage what it ought to be!"

It's the same way with relationships in God's family. Certainly the reality can fall far short of the ideal. But the ideal, laid out for us in Scripture, tells us what Christian relationships *can* be. And our response to problems in the church, as in the home, needn't be to give up and quit, but to put some effort into making our relationships with other Christians what they ought to be—and what they *can* be.

Why the breakdown?

When our church falls short of the ideal, it may be hard to realize what a great thing God has for us in other Christians. A high school guy, a new Christian, says, "I find it hard to fit in, or accept, some Christian kids because I can see so much hypocrisy in them. I would rather work for God in non-Christian circles than with Christian kids. Many kids in the church seem to come to church to meet others, to see their girls, to be able to say they were active in the youth group, to show off clothes, or because their parents make them come. It is very difficult to talk to kids like this because they think they've already made it."

Another, a girl, bitterly attacks her church friends: "I don't like them. They are always cliquey. I can do without them. I am definitely superior to them and they don't want me in their great group."

What makes for this kind of thing in a church group? What makes it hard for us to love and support each other?

"I found it hard to relate to Christian kids," says a college girl, "because they sometimes mocked or laughed at my beliefs. I expect this from non-Christians but not from Christians."

This kind of thing really is hard to take. Says a thoughtful nineteen-year-old from New York, "Many times in my relationships with other Christian kids, for instance at a youth gathering, a hint of skepticism is in the kids' attitudes toward each other. It seems as if everyone stands in judgment of everyone else, taking every opportunity to tear them apart. It's also been very hard for me to have serious discussions about my faith in Christ with other Christian young people, but after all, that's 'old stuff' and many young people treat it as such!"

Things like this—cliques that exclude others, an attitude of criticism and unconcern—drive persons apart. These work just the opposite of the forgiving, accepting, self-revealing ways that we've seen are necessary for coming closer to others. And because we Christians are in the same family, it's terribly serious when we drift apart. In fact, ways of living together that separate us as persons are the real cause of relationship breakdown in our churches, and this, in turn, is one of the biggest reasons why many youth and adults today aren't the growing, excited Christians they could be if only we'd live together in love, encouraging and helping each other.

It's because relationships are so important that the Bible makes plenty of blunt statements about wrong ways as well as right ways of living in the church. In fact, it says far more about *relating* than about what meetings the church holds, and when, and what to do at them. (In fact, it says next to *nothing* about *them!*) But it's plain and outspoken on our attitudes and actions toward each other.

> Don't criticize and speak evil about each other, dear brothers. If you do, you will be fighting against God's law of loving one another, declaring it is wrong. But your job is not to decide whether this law is right or wrong but to obey it. Only he who made the law can rightly judge among us. He alone decides to save us or destroy. So what right do you have to judge or criticize others? (James 4:11–12).

> You have no right to criticize your brother or look down on him. Remember, each of us will stand personally before the Judgment Seat of God. . . . So don't criticize each other any more. Try instead to live in such a way that you will never make your brother stumble by letting him see you doing something he thinks is wrong" (Rom. 14:10, 13).

> Don't grumble about each other, brothers. Are you yourselves above criticism? For see! The great Judge is coming. He is almost here. (Let him do whatever criticizing must be done.) (James 5:9)

One reason the negative as well as the positive sides of relationships are stressed in the Bible is that family relationships have tremendous power for hurting as well as for helping. The breakup of a home hurts the people in it because their lives are so bound up together. And when our relationships with other Christians break down, there is tremendous power to hurt ourselves and others spiritually. This power to hurt comes because we do in fact belong together. We are in the same family whether we're willing to accept and love each other or not, and our lives are bound up together too.

No wonder the Bible makes so much of relationships. "Warmly welcome each other into the church, just as Christ has warmly welcomed you," we are commanded in Romans (15:7). And in Colossians it says, "Be gentle and ready to forgive; never hold grudges. Remember, the

Lord forgave you, so you must forgive others. Most of all, let love guide your life, for then the whole church will stay together in perfect harmony" (3:13–14).

Most of all, let love guide your lives.

In living together with other Christians we are to learn how to "stay together in perfect harmony" because this *is* the way to get the help we each need to grow in our faith and as persons. And there is no substitute for what God has provided for us in each other.

The main point of all this discussion, then, is simple. We Christians *do* affect each other, for good or for bad. We can live together in God's way, and find an amazing closeness and a fantastic love that will recharge us and free us even more to love and help others. Or we can live together in wrong ways—criticizing instead of forgiving, judging instead of accepting, cutting ourselves off from each other instead of being open and honest. But if we do, we're in terrible danger. "If instead of showing love among yourselves you are always critical and catty, watch out!" the Bible warns. "Beware of ruining each other!" (Gal. 5:15).

Somehow, if things aren't right between the Christians you know, and between them and you, this is something that just *has* to be set right.

Summing up

Our relationships with other Christians are one of God's main supply lines, a source of strength and help for us in our own growing as persons and as His children. But life in God's family isn't always up to the ideal. Relationships can break down, cutting Christians off from each other. When this happens, we're cut off from the help we can draw from others.

How do we react if things aren't ideal in our churches?

If the pattern of relationships between those of us who make up one of Christ's assemblies of believers is off track? We can remember three important truths and learn to act on them.

Appearances can fool us. Your church may not look much like a high-powered fellowship from which love and concern can flow out to support you. But it *can* be like that. "So stop evaluating Christians by what the world thinks about them or by what they seem to be like on the outside," the apostle Paul warns. "Once I mistakenly thought of Christ that way, merely as a human being like myself. How differently I feel now!" And Paul goes on: "When someone becomes a Christian he becomes a brand new person inside. He is not the same anymore. A new life has begun!" (2 Cor. 5:16–17). What people may seem like—or be—isn't the whole story.

So no matter what the appearances, people who know Jesus Christ aren't to be judged "by what they seem to be like on the outside." God's power is there, inside. They can change, and things can change.

Attitudes can infect us. We all tend to respond to others and treat them the same way as they treat us. If the kids in church are critical and cutting, if they hold back their real selves and present only a phony front, the pressure is on us to act the same way. If the whole atmosphere of our relationships breathes criticism (and for some of the kids I've quoted, it seems to), we begin to be eaten by criticism too.

This is only natural. But we don't *have* to let criticism and phoniness infect us. Forgiveness and honesty still provide a way out for us—God's way out. But you or I are likely to slip into others' patterns of living if we're not aware of the danger, if we don't decide, no matter what, to live *our* lives God's way.

Attitudes can infect others. That's the other side of the coin. While the way others act toward us puts pressure on us to respond in kind, we can put that same kind of pressure *on them!* Instead of reacting to others' patterns, we can set the pattern for them to respond to. This is behind Paul's advice to Timothy, a young man who had to set the tone in the church of New Testament days: "Don't let anyone think little of you because you are young. Be their ideal; let them follow the way you teach and live; be a pattern for them in your love, your faith, and your clean thoughts" (1 Tim. 4:12).

If your church or your Christian friends aren't what they should be (and can be!), don't start griping about them. That's letting *them* set the pattern for you, and you'll soon be just as far off as they are. No, start by setting a new pattern. Start living with them in forgiving love. Accept them as they are, and take the risk of being—and revealing—yourself.

God's way of living in relationships is infectious too!

Steps to take

1. Think about relationships you have with other Christians, and especially with the young people at your church. Write a paragraph describing these relationships.

2. Take a look at the picture of "ideal" relationships given in Romans 12:3–15:7.
   a. How, specifically, does this ideal compare with the situation described in your paragraph?
   b. Find some ways in this passage that you can "set the pattern" of relationships for your Christian friends.

3. If you can think of two or three others who might

be especially interested in building toward the ideal with you, share what we've been thinking about in this book. An awful lot can happen when two or three get together!

9

Beyond friendship

All this talk about closeness and belonging sounds real good. Still, this idea of deep-down sharing between Christians raises other questions. Like that of a college girl, who asks, "How can I find a friend whom I can talk about important things with, and whom I can talk to when I have a problem? I've lots of acquaintances but I'd feel like I was imposing to tell them my problems. Also, I don't trust that they'd really understand or care."

It's a good question. How *do* we get beyond friendship to that "see how they love one another" relationship that marked so many in the early church?

Three years ago Jim, a dynamic young Californian, came into my office at Wheaton College. He'd read some of the things I was writing then about the church, and about our need for the helping, caring relationships discussed in this book. Since I'd written about sharing our real selves with others, he thought I knew how. So he began immediately to talk in a deeply personal way. He shared more than his ideas; he shared his feelings, his real self. And it scared me to death!

That's right. Instead of helping me open up, his honesty and willingness to reveal himself frightened me, and I pulled back into an impersonal shell.

I think that experience hurt both of us. He didn't know, I'm sure, that my writing then reflected only my awareness of a need for deeper fellowship, and not my ability to experience it.

I go back to this experience whenever anyone asks, "How can I find a friend to whom I can talk about important things?" Potentially each Christian—each brother and sister in Christ—is such a person. But many aren't yet ready to share themselves. So if I come on too strong I'm very likely to frighten the other person into withdrawal. Just as Jim frightened me.

This idea, that we all have to grow in our ability to relate as Christians, seems to be behind some advice the Bible gives us. It implies that until we grow and until others grow, our ventures in sharing may be misunderstood. They may be rejected, and we may be hurt. Notice what it says:

> Since you have been chosen by God who has given you a new kind of life, and because of his deep love and concern for you, you should practice tender-hearted pity and kindness to others. Don't worry about making a good impression on them but be ready to suffer quietly and patiently. Be gentle and ready to forgive; never hold grudges. Remember, the Lord forgave you, so you must forgive others (Col. 3:12–13).

Can we cut down on misunderstandings, and so minimize the need to forgive and be forgiven? Can we come close to each other without hurting or being hurt? Yes, if we remember that relationships are something we must *grow into,* not something we find.

This means that when we want to go beyond friendship

with other Christians, we need to seek ways to *develop* this kind of relationship with others—not look for a person with whom we can experience it immediately. And if we look at our problem as one of developing (not finding) Christian relationships, we can see several clear guidelines.

Offer, don't force, yourself. If you or I force ourselves on another person his response will almost always be to pull away. That's what happened when Jim came on too strong for me to take. I felt frightened, beyond my depth, and drew back.

How do we force ourselves on a person? Let's think about relationships as developing on different levels (see Fig. 1). For example, Level A might represent the

"stranger" level of friendship. Strangers talk together, but they don't feel closeness. Usually they discuss only surface issues, ones that don't hit them where they live. Level B is the "acquaintance" level. You may enjoy each other's company, discover things you have in common, and talk about mutual interests. Level C represents "friendship." Now closeness is felt, and some feelings as well as ideas are shared as you discover more and more of each other as real persons. Level D represents "close friendship." Here you share deeper feelings and experiences. Each cares for the other person and is sensitive to his feelings and needs. Each wants to help the other, and does. Level E represents the "Christian fellowship" relationship. Here believers not only share freely and fully, but are committed to each other. Each trusts the other enough to be utterly honest with him. And at the core of this relationship is a common commitment to Christ, and a common goal of living for Him. This is the real meaning of fellowship: to have all this in common because of Christ.

With this in mind, we can understand the idea of forcing ourselves on others. It's speaking on a C or D level to a person we only know in an A or B way. It's moving *too fast* in sharing yourself. Too fast for the other person to feel comfortable.

Actually, we are all free personalities and we don't like to be forced into things. We feel somehow that being pushed faster than we want to go violates our rights as a person. And it does! So when you or I move too fast with another person, he *rightly* reads that action as an attempt to force him into something. And he resists.

To build relationships, we have to give others the right to accept or reject our offer of friendship. We have no right to force them.

Figure 1

GOING DEEPER
A Pattern for Personal Relationship

Levels	Communication
A strangers ○	○ "say hi as he goes by"
B acquaintances ○	○ "stop and chat briefly"
C friends ○	○ "talk and get personal now and then"
D close friends ○	○ "share ourselves and our deep concerns"
E Christian fellowship ○○	"commit ourselves to each other in honesty and caring"

But do offer! It's hard to find balance here. How can we offer ourselves to others? How can we show them we're willing to come closer, without forcing ourselves on them? First, listen. Listen to them in the way described in chapter 2. That kind of listening says loud and clear, "I am interested in knowing you better." Second, venture out to open up the next level of relationship by sharing something on it. If you're chatting with an acquaintance, be willing to share some of your feelings as an invitation for him to enter your life more significantly. Third, remember that such invitations are accepted by a *response in kind.* If a person is willing to go deeper with you, he'll probably open himself up to you at the same level. If an acquaintance is interested in beginning a friendship, he'll respond by sharing some of his real self too.

Only when a person wants to move closer to you, and shows you in this way, should you consider staying on that deeper level of conversation.

Invite, but don't force.

It may take a while for such invitations to be understood or accepted. We may be rebuffed time and again. That's where forgiveness comes in. Because rebuffs do hurt. But we can afford to continue to "be gentle and ready to forgive." And we can afford to keep trying.

Sometimes a person will accept our invitation, and we'll grow close so quickly it will amaze us. But usually we *grow* into fellowship over a period of time. And often with ups and downs. But growth is like that. A baby doesn't crawl one day and do the hundred-yard dash the next! Learning to walk takes time. What's important is taking those first stumbling steps.

And that's what is important for you and me too. The way beyond friendship may be long for us, but let's dare to take the first steps.

All together

So far we've thought of beyond-friendship relationships as one-to-one experiences. You and one friend. Or maybe two. But there is also a beyond-friendship level of life for a group of Christians. For all of us, together. And closeness in our group of Christians, our church, is as important as closeness between individual believers. How about building real fellowship in your youth group. Or between teens and adults in your church? Seem like a pretty tall order? It is, but there are guidelines here, too. Let's look at some of them:

What unites us? People come together in groups for many reasons. Like, to play on a football team. Or to support a political party. Or to discuss great books. Things like these provide a basis for their association.

But church is different. As Christians we come together because of Jesus Christ. Ideally, we gather because we're committed to Him and to being His disciples. This is what the apostle Paul talks of when he encourages the Philippians

> always to live as Christians should, so that, whether I ever see you again or not, I will keep on hearing good reports that you are standing side by side with one strong purpose—to tell the Good News (Phil. 1:27).

He continues by showing this church how to live together in unity as Christians should:

> Is there any such thing as Christians cheering each other up? Do you love me enough to want to help me? Does it mean anything to you that we are brothers in the Lord, sharing the same Spirit? Are your hearts tender and sympathetic at all? Then make me truly happy by loving each other and agreeing wholeheartedly with each other, working together with one heart and mind and purpose. Don't be selfish; don't live to make a good impression on

> others. Be humble, thinking of others as better than yourself. Don't just think about your own affairs, but be interested in others, too, and in what they are doing (Phil. 2:1–4).

Earlier I said one reason for the breakdown of relationships in the churches is that we live together in the wrong way. We criticize instead of care, and judge instead of forgive. Here's another reason: we come together for the wrong reasons. I mean, why do we Christians get together? Sometimes it's just to have a good time. Sometimes to find friends of the opposite sex. Sometimes it's for Sunday school, or worship. Or club programs. All these are good. But underlying all, we get together to learn how to stand and work together as Christians. We need to share our lives and look together into the Bible to discover the meaning of life for us. We need to help each other grow as Christ's disciples. Since the source of our unity is Jesus Christ, we'll grow together and learn to love each other only when we share with each other how Christ relates to our lives, and when we commit ourselves to live individually and collectively for Him.

How different can we be? Whenever we think about unity and "wholeheartedly agreeing" with each other, this question comes up. Does living in fellowship with other Christians mean *conformity?* If most Christians part their hair in the middle, do I have to? If most of them don't like red, do I have to toss out my red clothes? If most won't play Monopoly (because they feel it's wrong), should I give it up too? Thoughts like this came out when one high schooler wrote, "It is always hard getting along with kids at church, even though this should be an easy area. There are conflicts about whether or not Christians should dance, etc. This is one relationship Christians really need to build up in their lives by having friends that share your religious views."

I really don't have any quarrel with a church agreeing on certain standards for reason of personal conviction. But we all ought to understand that there is room in the church for differences. In one place the Bible says, "Give a warm welcome to anyone who wants to join you as a member of the church, even though his faith is weak. Don't criticize him for having different ideas from yours about what is right and wrong" (Rom. 14:1). Of course the Bible is not talking here about what Scripture labels sin. It's talking about the ways we differ. But you are welcome in my church whatever your differences, because what counts is what we have in common—Christ—rather than our differences.

In general, the teaching can be summed up this way: (1) Everyone is personally responsible to Christ—so let him be. Don't try to make him see and do things your way. (2) Remember that bitterness or criticism about things like this hurt relationships. If necessary, be willing to give up your rights if what you do hurts another Christian. But don't insist on the other person changing if you are mature enough to love him as a person without getting hung up on the differences (3) Remember that what is important is unity in Christ, and that for harmony we focus on personal and group commitment to Jesus Christ. We don't focus on our differences of opinion or convictions. A sinful attitude of heart, while protecting a cherished conviction, can be just as destructive as holding a wrong conviction.

I bring this up here because when a group of Christians comes together, the easy way to unity seems to be to set up rules that those who want to be "in" have to keep. The hard way to unity is to ignore superficial differences and to work at getting to know each other as persons. It is to accept each other as we are, and love each other as we are, and thus discover our true unity, based on sharing our life in Jesus Christ.

But different we are. And to find that common core we need to accept each other and our differences, without judging. Because God says so. Even if a person's "faith is weak," he's to be welcome in our church, and not criticized for having ideas that differ from ours.

Why are we together? We've already said it. Because we *need* each other to grow as persons and as Christians. This is a big reason for accepting people into our fellowship as they are. Maybe they do have ideas that are wrong, or do some things they might better not do. But instead of making them live up to our rules before they can join our little club, God's way is to welcome them. And Jesus Christ, as Lord of each life, will reshape them as they grow up into His ways. And reshape us, too.

I hope what I'm trying to say is coming through. It's just this: *The ground rules for living together as a group of Christians are just the same as those for coming closer as individuals.* We have to live together in our groups in a forgiving, accepting, and self-revealing way if that group is to function as Christ's church.

Can we take the risk of living this way with other Christians? Surely, because we are bound together in Christ, and we need to find that unity by sharing our commitment to Him. Our differences aren't what is important; our relationship as brothers and sisters *is.* As we learn to live together as Christians, each of us grows in Christ, and He makes any changes necessary in our personalities, in our thoughts, and in our actions.

We may not like these ground rules of His, but they *are* His. And we can't change them without running into real trouble.

Off the bench

There's one particular dimension of being Christians together that I want to put in a special plug for. One that really marks us as getting off the bench onto God's playing field. What is it? Being honest with other Christians.

In chapter 2 I suggested that, like Paul, we need to be willing to reveal our real selves to others if we're going to come closer to them. Now I want to point out that this also means being honest about *them.* Revealing our feelings about the other person. On the one hand the Bible says, "Admit your faults to one another and pray for each other" (James 5:16). And on the other it says we should be "speaking the truth in love" (Eph. 4:15 AV).

> Stop lying to each other; tell the truth, for we are parts of each other and when we lie to each other we are hurting ourselves. If you are angry, don't sin by nursing your grudge. Don't let the sun go down with you still angry—get over it quickly; for when you are angry you give a mighty foothold to the devil (Eph. 4:25–27).

Revealing ourselves has two sides. We know we can misunderstand others and get angry with each other. When we do, it's only natural to hide these "bad" feelings and pretend everything is all right. Or even to deny any hard feelings while inside we're upset and nursing a grudge. But we are to bring things out into the open, in love, and get the issue between us settled.

You can get an idea of how important this is when you remember what Christ told His disciples: "When you are praying, forgive anyone you are holding a grudge against" (Mark 11:25). And in another place:

> If, while you are offering your gift at the altar, you should remember that your brother has something against

> you, you must leave your gift there before the altar and go away. Make your peace with your brother first, then come and offer your gift (Matt. 5:23–24 *Phillips*).

Somehow getting things right between Christians is so important that God wants us to interrupt talking to Him to make peace!

I think this is why we're told over and over in the New Testament, "Don't lie to each other." It's not that we'd try to cheat a fellow Christian. Or get him in trouble. It's just that we do tend to cover up bad feelings about each other, never realizing that the way to *get rid of them* is to be honest about them! Honest with ourselves and honest with each other.

Living this honestly with others would be impossible if we didn't understand forgiveness. We need it, each one, from others. My anger against you is often (even usually!) *my* fault, not yours. So in expressing my feelings honestly, I'm not condemning you. I'm sharing my weakness and asking help for dealing with it. Asking forgiveness when I need it, and showing I am willing to forgive when you need it.

In a fellowship of people who really do love each other, this kind of honest-sharing life is possible. And necessary.

Such relationships don't happen in a church overnight. Or by us coming on too strong. But if we'll take the risk of acting by God's rules when we come together as His church, they *will* come.

And finally? One last word. To grow together in our relationships with Christians, we need a shared commitment to God's Word. Why? Because here we hear God speak to us individually and as a group. And in shaping our lives to fit what God says in the Bible, we become His disciples. Sure, sharing our lives with each other is important. But we must let Christ share with us too.

One group of teens I know, who decided to be serious about their faith, found a good way. At first just four or five kids came on Friday nights to the home of an adult church member. In a few months there were forty packing out the living room. What did they do? Nothing special. For an hour they simply shared—talking personally and revealingly about school, their problems and their needs, and the good things that happened to them. Then they read the Bible. One read a verse and anyone could comment on it, or raise a question. Then the next verse was read, and the next. And they spent about an hour this way, thinking and talking through a Bible passage. And then they prayed.

Now, this isn't a magic formula. Three hours on Friday won't make your group into the kind of fellowship these kids have found. But the kind of life they found—of honest sharing, of mutual commitment to Christ and His Word, and deep concern for each other expressed in shared prayer—this is the real life of Christ's church. What they discovered is way beyond friendship. It's *living* the love of God.

And that's really great. That's where we all want to get—beyond friendship, to being real, and really loving. Right there is where God plans for His children to be.

Steps to take

1. One thing many people worry about is cliques. After reading this chapter, what do you think about them? Are these wrong in the youth group, or right? When might they be helpful, and when harmful?

If you're in a clique right now, what can you do to have a positive impact on all the kids at your church?

2. Adults are part of the church too. Ideally, youth and adults can move beyond friendship together! So how would you react to the college student who says, "In relating to adults one must keep an even temper and an open mind at all times. As adults face the young and rebellious there is an automatic 'trench warfare' or stalemate set up. Each combatant has his mind made up, his arguments outlined, ears plugged, and tongue wagging at both ends ready to go." Does it have to be like this? How can *you* help make it different?
3. Some passages that describe our relationship with other Christians are worth looking at closely: 1 John 2:1–11; 3:11–19; and 4:7–21.
4. What would happen if your youth group, or the adults and teens in your church, all read these last two chapters and sat down together to talk about them? Might be interesting.

10

God, you're great

There's one last relationship we need to review—the key one. It's with God. Why is it the key one? One high school girl sees it this way: "I've found that once I admitted to myself I wasn't communicating with God, and once I wanted to do something about it, I did start to communicate; and as soon as I did, my relationships with my girl friends and boys, and my parents and my brothers, improved drastically, and I was at peace with myself."

I've already said a lot about relating to God, back in chapters 3 and 4. But one or two things more need to be said. Because when we get our relationship with God straight, then we make some wonderful discoveries.

Last Thursday night we had a fight at our house. A week before one of the kids had dropped gum on our new sofa (the first good furniture we've had in fourteen years of marriage). And we laid down a rule. I said, "Don't chew gum in the house." And my wife echoed, "No gum in the house."

So Thursday while bringing my boys home from

school, I stopped at a little store. They wanted gum. We got it, but I told them again, "You can't chew it in the house." Later my daughter got hold of a piece and started to unwrap it in the living room. And did my wife get upset! I told her I'd told the boys they couldn't chew it in the house (what I thought we'd agreed on the week before), and she said they couldn't *bring* it in the house (what *she* thought we'd agreed on the week before)! She was hurt because I had apparently ignored her, and when she is ignored it makes her feel terribly unwanted and unimportant. And she was angry too.

We talked about it, but she still felt hurt and angry. Still, things were quieting down when my teenager jumped into the argument, on my side. He thought the whole thing about the gum was unfair anyway, and he was *sure* his mother was all wrong in her feelings about me. And that really did it!

Later that night when we sat down to read the Bible together, the atmosphere was pretty strained. So we had to talk about it again. My wife felt bitterly angry now—not at me, but at Paul. Things had really been settling down when he butted in, and she saw him as a trouble-maker who just likes to see people going at each other. (He has at times gotten things started between others—purposefully or not.) So finally, with both my son and my wife bitter and angry, I made them sit down and gave them a little lecture. I talked about how we have to live together in God's way. In forgiving love. Without criticizing or judging. Accepting each other as we are, the bad as well as the good.

And my wife began to grin.

Later she told me this: "I felt so angry inside. When you talked, I knew what you said was right; but I was so angry inside that I just couldn't do anything about it. He had no right to butt in and cause trouble like that, and I just couldn't forgive him. Then that silly grin started on my face. *I* didn't grin. It just started, and I could feel the anger washing away inside. And I knew I wasn't doing it, because I couldn't.

"And all I could do was sit there and think, over and over, *God, You're great! God, You're great! God, You're great!*"

What neither my wife nor my son could do to straighten themselves out, God could do. And He did. He washed away the anger, and He created in them the same forgiving love He extends to us in Christ.

This is why I can sit down and write a book like this—one that talks about ways of living together that are simply beyond you and me. Because I know it's true when the Bible says that

> the power of the life-giving Spirit—and this power is mine through Jesus Christ—has freed me from the vicious circle of sin and death. We aren't saved from sin's grasp by knowing the commandments of God, because we can't and don't keep them, but God put into effect a different plan to save us. He sent his own Son, in a human body like ours—except that ours are sinful—and destroyed sin's control over us by giving himself as a sacrifice for our sins. *So now we can obey God's laws* if we follow after the Holy Spirit and no longer obey the old evil nature within us (Rom. 8:2–4).

We *can* follow God's ways.

We can live like this—in love and concern and beyond friendship—because of the power of God within us. God really is great! And it's great to discover His work inside.

Discovery

How do we make this kind of discovery for ourselves?

We start by beginning our relationship with God on His terms. We accept the forgiveness and love He offers us in Jesus Christ.

Then we go on to grow in our relationship with Him. How? It is much like the way we grow in any relationship. We reveal ourselves to Him and look in the Bible to see how He has revealed Himself. We spend time with other Christians, moving beyond friendship to share and encourage each other in our faith. And we decide to live life by His rules.

Committing ourselves to live His way is the real meaning of a "life of faith." "You see," the Bible says about Abraham's faith, "he was trusting God so much that he was willing to do whatever God told him to" (James 2:22). And this is just the kind of trust it takes if we're going to grow close to God. "When you obey me," Jesus said, "you are living in my love, just as I obey my Father and live in his love" (John 15:10).

And because of God's power within—because God really is great—you and I can live close to Him. We can live in His love.

That's why this book is on fitting in. A big part of living life God's way is living with others—with our parents, our acquaintances, with non-Christians, and with other believers.

You see, people are important to God.

And people should be important to you and me. How important? The Bible says, "Keep right on loving others as long as life lasts, so that you will get your full reward. Then, knowing what lies ahead for you, you won't become bored with being a Christian, nor become spiritually dull and indifferent, but you will be anxious to follow the example of those who receive all that God has promised them because of their strong faith and patience" (Heb. 6:11–12).

So there it is. God has planned a great life for you and me. A meaningful life. A life to be lived loving others. Try it, and you won't be bored with being a Christian. Oh, no! Not at all. You'll find yourself joining in and saying it too:

"God, you're great! Just great!"

Steps to take

1. If you want to strengthen your relationship with

God, read over chapters 3 and 4 again. How would you apply these principles to your devotional life?

2. There is a lot more to living close to God than I've been able to say in this short book. If you want more, you might look at the last few chapters of two earlier "Answers for Youth" books: *How I Can Be Real* and *How I Can Experience God.*

3. How can you step out, now, and trust God so much that you'll try His way of relating? Look back at the chart on page 121. Now list beside each level the names of those persons you feel you know that well.
   Choose one person with whom you want a closer relationship at each level, and go back over the book to get specific ideas on how you'll build with each.

Notes

Chapter 1

[1]About 2,000 Christian high school and college students contributed their thoughts and experiences to help create this book. You'll find them quoted throughout it, and every quote is authentic, reproduced here just as they said or wrote it.

[2]Joseph Katz et al., *No Time for Youth* (San Francisco: Jossey-Bass, 1969), p. 44.

Chapter 2

[1]Bruce Larson, *Dare to Live Now!* (Grand Rapids: Zondervan, 1965), p. 45.

[2]Moris Rosenberg, *Society and the Adolescent Self-Image* (Princeton, N.J.: U. Press, 1965), p. 184.

[3]Joost A. Merloo, "Communication and Mental Contagion," in L. Thayer, ed., *Communication: Concepts and Perspectives* (New York: Spartan, 1966), p. 5.

Chapter 4

[1]Bruce Larson, *Dare to Live Now!* (Grand Rapids: Zondervan, 1965), p. 41.

Chapter 5

[1]Lawrence Schaimberg, "Some Socio-Cultural Factors in Adolescent-Parent Conflict: A Cross-Cultural Comparison of Selected

Cultures," *Adolescence,* Vol. 4, No. 15 (Fall, 1969), p. 333.

[2]Reported in "We're Scared of Our Kids," a readers' poll, "Voice of Women" column, *Ladies Home Journal,* n.d.

Chapter 7

[1]For an extended discussion of how to stand up to social pressure and do what you believe is right—and how this will affect your standing with other kids—you might want to look at chapter 5 of *How I Can Be Real.*